THE MYSTIC ARTS
OF THE
NINJA

THE MYSTIC ARTS
OF THE
NINJA

HYPNOTISM, INVISIBILITY, AND WEAPONRY

STEPHEN K. HAYES

CONTEMPORARY
BOOKS

CHICAGO

Library of Congress Cataloging in Publication Data

Hayes, Stephen K.
  The mystic arts of the ninja.

  Includes index.
  1. Ninjutsu.   I. Title.
UB271.J3H38   1985   355.5'48   85-434
ISBN 0-8092-5343-7

Published by Contemporary Books, Inc.
Two Prudential Plaza, Chicago, Illinois 60601-6790
Manufactured in the United States of America
International Standard Book Number: 0-8092-5343-7

CONTENTS

ACKNOWLEDGMENT/ix

1
REKISHI
HISTORY'S MESSAGE OF SIGNIFICANCE/1

2
FU NO KATA
FIGHTING LIKE THE WIND/4

3
NINJA ARUKI
THE STEALTHY TREAD OF THE NINJA/31

4
NIN GU
NINJA TOOLS/55

5
IN-TON
CONCEALMENT AND CAMOUFLAGE FOR THE NINJA/101

6
SHURIKEN
NINJA THROWING BLADES/119

7
SAIMINJUTSU
THE NINJA'S POWER OF DIRECTING THE MIND/133

AFTERWORD
NINJUTSU TRAINING OPPORTUNITIES/143

INDEX/145

This book is dedicated to
Koyu Tanaka
whose generous friendship and support
helped to make my years
of apprenticeship in Japan possible.

Author Stephen K. Hayes, his wife Rumiko, and Dr. Masaaki Hatsumi, grandmaster of the ninja tradition.

ACKNOWLEDGMENT

As a small child of only five years old, I knew that it would be my destiny to be a part of the warrior tradition. Of course, at that age I hardly knew the words that would later be used to describe the outward manifestation of my quest through the realms of material and spiritual power.

It took me twenty years of steady searching to find at last the teacher who could guide me to the knowledge I had sought. In a small Japanese inn tucked away in the center of Noda City, Japan, I at last had the opportunity to meet Dr. Masaaki Hatsumi, headmaster of Bujinkan dojo and grandmaster of the ninja tradition. After that first night's brief introduction, I knew I could never ever go back to what I had been taught as the martial arts before that night, and there made a personal commitment that I would pursue that man's art throughout whatever it would take to achieve mastery. Little did I know that it would require an almost total realigning of my perceptions of all that is, and would require a lifetime of work before mastery could even begin to be realized.

This volume and indeed the entire series of which it is a part, is therefore an acknowledgment of my appreciation for all that has been shown and given to me by my teacher, Dr. Masaaki Hatsumi. Unique among master teachers of the warrior arts, all that he has attained in the way of enlightenment along the martial path serves to ever inspire those who would follow along after him.

THE MYSTIC ARTS
OF THE
NINJA

Ando Hiroshige woodbock print showing the mountain and marsh area of Iga Ueno, famed birthplace of the ninja warrior tradition of feudal age Japan.

1
REKISHI
HISTORY'S MESSAGE OF SIGNIFICANCE

The legendary warriors of feudal Japan known as the *ninja* were a manifestation of a unique set of cultural, economic, religious, and social pressures that stretched, buckled, and twisted across the remote island nation for hundreds of years during the first half of the current millenium. In an extended age of continuous civil warfare, broken only by an occasional stretch of unification that was most often characterized by severe regimentation and enforced obedience to the temporary central power, it is only natural for an art dedicated to physical and spiritual survival in the face of all odds to have materialized. In the history of feudal Japan, that art of underground resistance and self-direction came to be known as *ninjutsu*, or, as the method is commonly referred to today, the art of invisibility.

The art of ninjutsu, or *nin-po* as it is known in its higher order as a system of life guidance, has its roots in a broad collection of previous traditions that all had their own respective singular effects on the history and culture of Japan. According to a history of the art of ninjutsu as published by the Mie Prefecture Iga-Ueno City Ninja Museum and Library, and included in ninjutsu grandmaster Masaaki Hatsumi's book *Ninja/Ninpo Gaho* ("Ninja and Ninpo Illustrated"; Tokyo, Akita Shoten Publishers, 1964), the ancient Japanese *shinobi* discipline stems from roots emerging from a blending and meshing of

Japanese *shinto* ("divine spirit way") animistic beliefs, *kiaijutsu* ("art of harmonizing with the universal force"), *rekigaku* study and interpretation of astrological influences, *jojutsu* staff and cane fighting, and Chinese military tactics and strategy. According to the Iga document, from these roots grew the emerging trunk of Japanese *shugendo* mountain ascetic power cultivation, *bujutsu* sciences of individual combat, *heiho* military strategy, the refinements of *yamabushi* ("seekers in the mountains") *heiho* commando warfare tactics, and eventually the cultivation of the art of ninjutsu as a distinct discipline of personal self-protection.

DEVELOPMENT OF NINJUTSU

The original teachings and principles of the art of ninjutsu were developed through an experiential knowledge of combat methods, human psychology and cultural patterning, and the workings of natural phenomena and a personal closeness with nature. From this broad spectrum of considerations, the feudal Japanese science of survival under any circumstances eventually took its shape. The art came to be known as a countercultural opposite to the conventional concepts of warfare and territorial expansion that were routine during the feudal ages in ancient Japan.

The Japanese language written character for

1

忍

The Japanese written character for *"nin"* of ninja and ninjutsu, also pronounced as *shinobu*, is made up of two lesser characters for "blade" above and "heart" below.

nin of ninja, ninjutsu, and nin-po, reflects the nature of the art and the needs that caused it to come into being. Formed of two lesser characters, the upper part meaning "blade," and the lower part meaning "heart" or "spirit," the character means "stealth" and "secretness," as well as "endurance," "perseverance," and the quality of "putting up with." Though unenlightened critics of the art like to point out that the written character for *nin* gives the appearance of the ninja putting the blade above the heart in importance, implying that the ninja were heartless in the use of force, this gross misunderstanding is a perversion of the true meaning of the concept. More accurately the character *nin* suggests, "Although the enemy holds his blade menacingly over my heart, I will endure and eventually prevail."

CULTURAL STEREOTYPING

Much like the native North American Indian culture in the nineteenth-century United States, the true story of the feudal Japanese ninja families has been greatly misunderstood for the past several centuries. It must be remembered that the official historians who were responsible for recording the accounts of the times were, of course, always a part of the established military dictatorships. Therefore, any potential reference to the resistance shown by the oppressed families of Iga or Koga provinces would naturally be couched in the most derogatory of terms. The little that was recorded regarded the ninja families as criminals, terrorists, and assassins. As a counterbalancing perspective, it is enlightening to recall that those same brutal descriptions could also have been used by the eighteenth-century British to describe those persons that American schoolchildren are taught to regard as the bold and heroic founding fathers of the United States of America. Likewise, when reading tales that brand the ninja as cold assassins and spies for hire, modern students of history should bear in mind the penchant of keepers of the status quo for describing any person or thing in opposition in the most disparaging of terms.

In a nonpolitical overview, the following listing includes some of the more famous of Japan's legendary ninja heroes, with a brief note on each. In this listing, names are presented in the traditional Japanese format, with the family name appearing first, followed by given name.

Hattori Hanzo

The histories of Japanese ninjutsu most often refer to Hanzo as the most successful *jonin* (ninja group chief) of the Iga-gumi organization. Also known as Watanabe Hanzo and Yari no Hanzo ("Hanzo of the spear"), Hattori Hanzo gained his greatest fame at the time of the Honnoji no Hen incident in June of 1582. Tokugawa Ieyasu, later

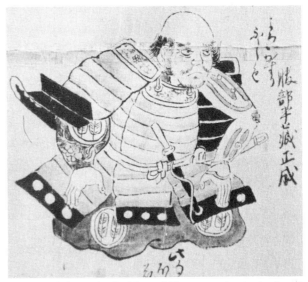

Iga ryu ninjutsu jonin Hattori Hanzo, as he is depicted in an historical text illustration.

to become the shogun to unify all Japan, was staying in Sakai near Osaka at the time of Oda Nobunaga's assassination. With Hanzo's ablity to quickly unite and organize over 300 ninja from both the Iga and Koga areas, Ieyasu was able to escape from Sakai and safely return to Okazaki castle, passing through what could have otherwise been a most dangerous stretch of territory in the Iga region.

After Honnoji no Hen, all details concerning the movements and actions of the regional *daimyo* (military rulers) and even the emperor were reported to Ieyasu by Hanzo. The vast extent and power of Hanzo's massive network surprised even Ieyasu. Hanzo later was appointed as the head of rear gate security for shogun Tokugawa Ieyasu's Edo Castle. To this day, the gate is still referred to as *Hanzomon*, or "Hanzo's gate." The Iga ryu jonin died at age 55 in 1596.

Momochi Sandayu

Legend tells that Sandayu was the teacher of Ishikawa Goemon, the famous bandit hero of feudal Japan. Sandayu is also known as one of the founders of Iga ryu ninjutsu, although there are few recorded details concerning his life. There are many theories as to his true identity. Some historians believe that he is the same person as jonin Momochi Tanba Yasumitsu, but this cannot be verified. Another theory has it that Sandayu was the nephew of Momochi Tanba Yasumitsu. Yet another theory has it that Sandayu was the same person as Fujibayashi Nagato. Momochi Sandayu is said to have been killed in the battle of

Village of Hojiro, out of which Momochi Sandayu's ninja group was based.

Tensho Iga no Ran. The Momochi family's descendants live in the Nabari region of Iga to this day.

Fujibayashi Nagato

Legend has it that Fujibayashi was head of Iga ryu ninjutsu along with Momochi Tanba. Fujibayashi was not known to have played a major role in the battle of Tensho Iga no Ran, in which Iga was invaded by Oda Nobunaga's troops in 1581, and there is not much information about him in the *Iranki* volume (history of the Tensho Iga no Ran battle). Fujibayashi is thought to be

Eihoji temple, with which the Momochi clan maintained a strong relationship.

Gravesite of ninjutsu jonin Fujibayashi Nagato, located on the grounds of the Shokakuji temple, of Higashiyubune, Ayamacho.

Fujibayashi's seventeenth century *Bansenshukai*, a
ten-volume collection of ninjutsu history,
personalities, and tactics from feudal Iga province.

related to Iga ryu ninjutsu's Hattori family.
Because of a similarity in the Buddhist posthum-
ous names of Fujibayashi Nagato and Momochi
Sandayu, some historians suspect that Fujibayashi was really Momochi, but there is no proof of
this theory. Perhaps Fujibayashi has gained the
major part of his fame due to the work of a later
descendant, Fujibayashi Yasutake, who in the
summer of 1676 compiled the famous *Bansenshukai* ("Ten Thousand Rivers Collect in the Sea")
ten-volume reference work on the techniques and
practice of ninjutsu in Iga.

Mochizuki Chiyome

Chiyome was the wife of Mochizuki Moritoki,
who was killed in the battle of Kawanakajima in
September of 1561. Chiyome's husband Moritoki
was the lord of Mochizuki Castle in Kitasaku
Province in Nagano, and his family tree included
Koga ryu ninja.

After her husband's death, Chiyome retired to
an old house in Nezu village of Nagano's Shinshu
Chiisagata Province. She was then asked to become the head of a *miko* (female shinto shrine
attendant) ninja spy ring operating in the Kai and
Shinano areas. Chiyome gathered orphaned and
runaway girls from different areas, and trained
them as miko vestal virgins while also training
them as *kunoichi* female ninja agents for the
Takeda family. The *kunoichi* jonin carefully
judged talents, attributes, and attractiveness of

each of the girls and placed them in appropriate
areas of operation.

Fuma Kotaro

Born in Sagami Prefecture, Kotaro was the
fifth generation jonin head of Fuma ryu ninjutsu.
He and his 200 followers, called *rappa* or *suppa*
("battle disrupters"), worked as a guerrilla band
in support of Odawara's Hojo family. Fuma
Kotaro's most famous battle was in March of
1581, when the massive troops of Takeda Shingen's son Katsuyori attacked the Hojo stronghold. Takeda set up his fortress in Ukishimaga-
hara, and the Hojo set up camp across the
Osegawa River from them. The Fuma group
crossed the river and attacked the Takeda troops
several times at night, and drove the Takeda
camp into disorder with their ninja tactics.

The story of the battle is written in the *Hojo
Godaiki* volume. By the time of the Tokugawa
Shogunate, however, the Fuma group had degen-
erated into a gang of pirates operating in the
Inland Sea.

Iga Ueno's Ookaji temple, located near Hattori
family's village, contains a statue of the eleven-faced
Juichimen Kannonzo, said to be the guardian spirit of
Koga Saburo Kaneie.

Saiga Magoichi

Born with the family name of Suzuki, Magoichi was head of the Kishu Saiga ninja group. A
master of Tsuda ryu *kajutsu* explosives and firearm methods as well as Saiga ryu ninjutsu,
Magoichi based his headquarters on Saiga Cape,

Gravesite of Shiroto Hachibei, an Iga ninja best known for his unsuccessful attempt on the life of Oda Nobunaga. Hachibei's grave is marked by a statue of En no Gyoja, the legendary seventh-century founder of *shugendo* (mountain ascetic power cultivation), said to have been worshipped by Shiroto Hachibei.

and recruited his men from the group of *jizamurai* (local samurai) from the vicinity of Saiga Castle. They possessed 2,000 rifles, a large and very valuable collection at that time, and they had many good marksmen; therefore, many regional lords courted their favor and support.

Magoichi was involved in the battle of Naniwa Kanzakigawa Gassen, in which the ninja's arch rival Oda Nobunaga, also took part. Saiga Magoichi employed the tactic of *shaki no jutsu* "flag discarding" to win the battle. The Saiga group left their own battle flags behind and moved into position carrying copies of the flag of their enemy Nobunaga, who saw his own flags and thought them his allies. In that age of Japanese history, tactics that violated the accepted codes of honorable warfare were considered scandalous and cowardly, but the countercultural ninja families were prohibited from engaging in self-protection combat anyway, and therefore could do anything. Magoichi's standard strategies were surprise attacks coupled with highly effective firearm tactics.

A pious Buddhist, Saiga Magoichi continued to fight Oda Nobunaga, the oppressor of Buddhism, up to the time of his death.

Suginobo Minsan

Born Tsuda Minsan Kanmotsu, he adopted the monk name Suginobo Minsan. Legends say that he was the founder of Negoro ryu ninjutsu, and was highly skilled at using firearms.

Minsan's brother is also a famous personage in the history of the introduction of firearms to Japan in the late 1500s. Minsan heard rumor of firearms being demonstrated at Tanegashima, and traveled from Negoro to visit Tanegashima. Suginobo Minsan was presented a *koshizashi* ("hip-held gun"), which he took to a blacksmith to have copies made. Thereafter, the *sohei* military monks were proud of their shooting techniques, and were reputed to be as skilled as the famous Saiga ninja group marksmen.

In March of 1585, Toyotomi Hideyoshi attacked Negoro temple with a massive 25,000-troop force, because in the previous year Hideyoshi had been soundly defeated by the Negoro group. Minsan fought valiantly, but faced Mashita Nagamori who ultimately defeated and killed him.

Sugitani Zenjubo

Zenjubo was the oldest son of Sugitani Yototsugu, who was the jonin head of one of the 53 Koga ninja families. Zenjubo was good with firearms, and was recruited by Rokkaku Takayori as a sniper against the conqueror Oda Nobunaga. On May 19, 1570, Zenjubo lay in wait for Nobunaga and shot at him with two bullets, but the bullets hit Nobunaga's shoulder padding only and did not injure the notoriously cruel general.

Muryojufukuji temple, located in Iga Ueno's Shimokobe area, was the staging point for Iga ryu ninja who eventually overcame Oda Nobuo, Nobunaga's son, and took control of his fortress in Maruyama. Their victory was to be short lived, however, as Nobuo's powerful father then invaded Iga in the devastating Iga no Ran battle campaign.

Sugitani Zenjubo then fled into the mountains of Omi Prefecture to hide.

After four years of evading his enemy, he was finally captured. Nobunaga had Zenjubo tortured until he confessed and revealed the plot proposed by Rokkaku. The Koga ninja was then executed by means of a hideous torture that took six days to produce death.

Kato Danjo

It is thought that Kato was a ninja of the Iga ryu, as his name appears in the book *Omikoku Yoshiryaku* ("Brief History of Omi Province"). There is also a popular theory that he was born in Ibaraki Prefecture. Danjo's ninja nickname was *Tobikato*, or "jumping Kato," as he was considered to be a master of ninjutsu leaping and jumping methods.

Home of Sawamura family, members of the Iga ryu ninja group. Typical of feudal age Japanese ninja home construction, the Sawamura house features a moat and stone retaining wall to help ensure privacy.

In an attempt to gain a high position in the warlord Uesugi Kenshin's troops, he approached Kenshin and demonstrated his ninja *genjutsu* arts of illusion. Kenshin wanted to further test him, so Kato used his skills of invisibility to enter surreptitiously the castle of one of Kenshin's top generals and remove a valuable scroll and one of the servant girls. After he found that Uesugi was still reluctant to employ him, he went to rival lord Takeda Shingen to seek employment. Takeda was also reluctant to hire him, suspecting that he was being set up by a double agent from the Uesugi camp. Takeda is said to have secretly ordered his

retainer Tsuchiya Heihachiro to kill Kato as a means of ending the controversy and dilemma.

Kido Yazaemon

In the autumn of 1579, this Iga ryu ninja and firearms expert organized a clandestine attempt at assassinating Oda Nobunaga, the sworn enemy of all ninja. The plot was ultimately unsuccessful, but the incident is recorded in the *Iranki* volume on the campaign to conquer Iga, and Kido's name is included in the account.

Igasaki Dojun

Though the dates of Dojun's birth and death are uncertain, it is known that he was born in Tateoka of Iga Province, so people called him Tateoka no Dojun. Igasaki Dojun is said to have

Ruins of the farm house of the Mando family, said to be among the top students of Iga ryu ninjutsu founder Igasaki Dojun.

been the original founder of what later became known as the forty-nine ninjutsu ryu of Iga, and Dojun's story is recorded in the first volume of the *Bansenshukai* record of the practice of Iga ryu ninjutsu.

Rokkaku Yoshitaka, of Sasaki in the Omi region, engaged Dojun's help in the difficult task of defeating Dodo, who had betrayed Rokkaku. Dojun took forty-four Iga ninja and four Koga ninja with him and set out to bring victory to the Rokkaku camp. As a means of breaking into the enemy's stronghold, it is said that Dojun and his men used a paper lantern with the enemy's family crest painted on it, and also employed the ninja's *bakemonojutsu* "ghost arts" to go on and accomplish the necessary.

Kumawaka

Born in the Chiisagata Prefecture of Shinshu, Kumawaka ("young bear") is thought to have been a *genin* (operative agent) of a Koga ryu ninjutsu family in league with Takeda Shingen. The Takeda family had a force of seventy *suppa* (another term for ninja guerillas), and out of that seventy, thirty were assigned in groups of ten to three of Shingen's generals. They could then split up the target area for systemized information gathering.

In the battle of Wariga Toge in 1561, Kumawaka's general Iidomi Toramasa split his troops into two units, but then discovered that he had forgotten to bring his battle flags. A known

Iga home of Kizu Echizen, connected to the powerful Taira family that opposed the Minamoto, who eventually took control of Japan as Shogun. The Kizu were a prominent family in the area, known for their work in sponsoring temple and shrine festivals and holiday celebrations. The house takes good advantage of the mountainous terrain on which it was built, and is attached to a small, concealed fortress in the mountain ridges above it.

master of ninjutsu stealth and running methods, Kumawaka ran all the way back to the Iidomi stronghold, got the flags, and returned to their battlefield camp, all within four hours' time. Also accomplished within that four-hour period was the task of secretly breaking into his own castle to get the flags, since the guards at the gate did not recognize the undercover agent as one of their own warriors.

At around the same time as the battle, Shingen's prized book, the *Kokin Wakashu*, was stolen, and somehow Kumawaka was suspected of the theft. In order to remove himself from suspicion, Kumawaka went out on his own, found the real thief, and brought him back with Takeda's book.

Ishikawa Goemon

Though none of the ninja families of Iga or Koga would call him one of their own because of his reputation for using the methods of ninjutsu to aid him in stealing for his own personal gain, no history of legendary Japanese ninja names would be complete without that of Ishikawa Goemon. There are many theories as to where he was born, but no concrete information. Three popular theories regarding Goemon's birthplace include Hamamatsu in Enshu, Oshu's Shirakawa, or Ishikawa Village of Iga Province.

Thought to have originally been a genin agent of Iga ryu ninjutsu, Goemon was killed on August 24, 1594, the legends claiming that he was boiled to death in oil. Though Ishikawa Goemon's name is not listed in the *Bansenshukai* written record of Iga ryu ninjutsu, the notorious bandit hero appears often in the world of novels and theater as the greatest thief in the history of Japan.

LIMITED CONVENTIONAL VIEWS

It is of great significance to note that the general world's observation of the impact of the art of ninjutsu seems to be limited to that narrow portion of Japanese history that led up to and included the *Sengoku Jidai* Warring States period that ended in the late 1500s. Therefore to many Japanese and now westerners as well, imaginative tales of the Hattori family, "Monkey-Jump" Sasuke, "Concealing Mist" Saizo, and the amoral Goemon, comprise the entire image of the ninja and their arts. The *shinobi* realm is thought to be a dark one, revolving around moonlit nights, black suits and masks, scandalous tactics of duplicity, and ingeniously concealed tools for the murdering of enemies.

As an unfortunate by-product of the media's portrayal of Japan's ninja legacy, some modern martial artists now shy away from possible involvement in the practice of ninjutsu for fear that they will be forced to involve themselves in activities requiring them to change or give up religious beliefs, pledge allegiance to subversive political cadres, or conceal their true-life personalities through underground cover identities. So-called "traditionalists" in the martial arts attempt to dismiss ninjutsu by trying to convince others that the art is really a collection of brutal, immoral, or even cowardly methods. Conventional martial sport competitors have publicly ridiculed the teachers of authentic Japanese ninjutsu as being only capable of offering lessons in "how to

A few of the dozens of Japanese children's books that have presented the art of ninjutsu in the light of cultural fantasy. Though generations of Japanese have grown up to the delights of storybook ninja tales, the blending of fact with greatly exaggerated fiction has done much to confuse the perceptions of western world martial artists regarding the authentic ninjutsu warrior training system of life arts. In the orient, the popular image of the ninja is one of the sorcerer and illusionist; in the west the prevalent image seems to be that of the assassin in black. The little-known reality is that neither of the exaggerated myths comes anywhere close to reflecting the true essence of ninja warrior enlightenment.

hide," as compared with the more manly goals of how to beat others in contest arenas. After one has had the opportunity to be exposed to the true essence of the *shinobi* warrior's lifeways, however, it is easy to see through the falsehoods of all these common misunderstandings.

To obtain a proper perspective regarding the art of the ninja warriors of Iga and Koga, one must view the phenomena through an expanded perception of the totality of history's timeline. The impartial critic would not judge the validity of the Christian religion solely on the basis of priestly brutality in the hellish days of the Inquisition during the Dark Ages. Nor would he judge the good-heartedness of the American people solely on the basis of Congressional acts that stripped the Japanese-ancestored United States citizens of property and condemned them to primitive desert concentration camps during the 1940s. Therefore, neither will the impartial critic restrict his or her ideas regarding the value of the ninja warrior ways to the whimsical coverage provided by the limited scope of the popular media.

TRUE SIGNIFICANCE

The wisdom and perspective of the ninja actually stretches back centuries before the 1400s and 1500s so often thought of as the age of the ninja's greatest influence on Japanese history. In the middle of the seventh century, the legendary En no Gyoja is credited with the founding of shugendo warrior ascetic training, and the prince Shotoku is said to have employed the first ninja as a means of gaining broader legal and human perspectives before sitting in judgment of the subjects he ruled. Both Iga and Koga were wilderness areas, ignored for the most part and left to themselves by the ruling powers of the island nation of Japan.

By the late 900s, refugees from the collapse of the T'ang dynasty in neighboring China had made their way to the Iga and Koga regions seeking sanctuary, and were welcomed and accepted by the locals inhabiting the area. In the late 1100s, the establishment of the Minamoto family's Kamakura shogunate produced, as an offshoot, the establishment of the Togakure ryu of ninjutsu by one of the survivors of the battles that eventually decimated the Taira clan.

It was only during the incredible sadness, violence, and oppression of the buildup leading to the tragic Sengoku Jidai Warring States Period that the warriors history would later call ninja were forced to rely almost entirely on the subtle realms of underground resistance in order to survive. Unlike the established samurai families who by law and cultural pressure were forced to conduct their affairs in alignment with set codes of action and speech—even if those codes meant walking into certain death by suicide—the ninja families were deprived of the right to legally defend themselves, and thereby were granted the total freedom of choice available only to those who face life with nothing else to lose. This temporary demand of history, however, does not in any way imply that the art of ninjutsu is limited entirely to the crafts of espionage, commando tactics, and guerrilla warfare. What is implied instead is the fact that the ninja warriors of Iga and Koga were just as capable of approaching endurance from the dark side of universal power as the bright side when the survival of their families was in the balance.

Therefore, it should be remembered that the ninja warrior is the epitome of spiritual freedom and power, able to tread confidently when necessary on either side of the nebulous fine line that separates the light from the darkness. Though popular misconception branded the ninja as the warrior of darkness, he is in truth the bearer of the universal light in a world that sometimes grows dim. Because he carries a brilliant light in the center of his heart, he can dwell in the light without coming to depend on being there, just as he can move through the realms of darkness without being overcome and rendered unable to escape once his purpose has been served.

This then is the essence of all paths of warrior wisdom, regardless of the label with which the practitioners choose to brand their individual arts. Through the choice to confront the path of challenge, to continuously face risks, to explore the very edge of defeat to better know triumph, the warrior discovers the keys to the universal power that seems to charge both the brightness and the darkness in the same manner. As he further discovers his place in the thread of the scheme of universal totality, the enlightened warrior eventually attains the freedom that affords him the insight to see that, ultimately, there is no separation whatsoever between what the fearful differentiate as the realms of light and dark, good and evil. In truth, this universal oneness is the key to the puzzle that mankind has sought to solve since the very beginnings of thought.

2
FU NO KATA
FIGHTING LIKE THE WIND

The only way to win in most competitive sports is to train hard and well in preparation for the contest, have a thorough grounding in the rules and strategies that will lead to victory, engage the opponent firmly, throw off his attempts to score against you, move aggressively towards scoring against him, and keep working at it valiantly until you succeed or time runs out. This general advice rings true for all competitions from chess tournaments to football games to kickboxing matches. It is, in fact, difficult to think of any popular sport or game for which this admonition would not be appropriate.

Successful self-protection is another matter altogether, and the methods that are often the most effective for handling dangerous assailants can run in total contradiction to the coaching suggestions that would bring sports victories. Few would argue with the fact that a competitor who is poorly prepared when compared to his opponent, has fewer skills and commands less power, avoids confrontation at all times, makes no attempt to score, breaks as many rules as he can, and attempts to end the contest as quickly as possible by any means, would stand little chance of ever winning in the conventional sense of the word. It is difficult to even think of a sports event that could be won under those conditions. And yet it is often just those conditions that permit a smaller, less hostile, and perhaps outnumbered or

disadvantaged individual to successfully defend himself on the street or in the field.

Why then do so many martial arts training instructors insist on coaching their students in methods of sportsmanship while claiming to be teaching skills of self-protection? It probably has a lot to do with the strongly rooted American sense of fairness, the fact that the majority of the oriental martial arts taught today were specifically designed as sports or art systems and not as combat methods, that there is probably more money and excitement in sport martial arts tournament training, and—to be totally honest—because few parents are comfortable with the idea of their children actually learning realistic life-saving methods that, of course, conflict with the conventional social programming dispensed by schools and religions.

When leaving behind ideas of weight classifications, skill-level designations for contenders, safety factors, definitions of scoring methods, and considerations of how to present an event that will excite and involve spectators, you begin to enter the realm of combat reality training. In any instance of street survival self-defense, it is highly likely that you will be confronted with an assailant who is bigger, stronger, and faster than you, and who has some sort of advantage, be it the element of surprise, possession of a superior weapon, heightened pain tolerance through drugs or insanity, accomplices for backup support, or at least some more experience at actually killing, maiming, and/or terrifying others. Despite all the odds, however, you still have to win. You either go home healthy and happy or you do not. There is no such thing as "second place" in a street fight or field attack.

The authentic Japanese art of ninjutsu evolved from the need for pragmatic self-protection under difficult odds in a time of continuous civil warfare. Ironically, this model of reality is still highly appropriate for our modern society with its ever-upward-spiraling violent crime rates and ever-broadening net of legal restrictions on what a citizen is permitted to do in order to protect his or her home and family. Unlike the time of the glorified stories of the American Old West, where superior firepower, a lot of grit, and being faster on the draw constituted what was necessary for survival and social stability, contemporary standards demand a more thoughtful approach to guarantee successful outcomes in confrontation situations.

One of the many options for handling an attack under the methods taught by the Bujinkan dojo ninja training halls today is the art of evasion. Though running contrary to the requirements for creating an exciting sports event, moving and thinking like the wind is sometimes the only way to successfully handle a violent attacker. By not being where the assailant expects you to be, and not moving in the manner that the assailant has learned to anticipate, you can increase the likelihood of not being where his punches, kicks, grabs, or cuts want to go. Evasive movement also allows for a realistic method of handling blows from stronger attackers that would be difficult to stop with conventional bone-and-muscle power blocking techniques.

In the ninja's *fu no kata* wind-like mode of response, circular and slipping motions take obvious head and body targets out of the expected zones of interception, while simultaneously setting up the defender for a scientific counterattack against targets that the attacker might not be aware of as being vulnerable. Incoming strikes, grabs, hits, or cuts are not "defended against" as such, but rather are avoided or not permitted to effectively contact their target. Realignment and redirection replace resistance in grappling encounters, allowing the smaller victim to overcome the advantages of the large attacker. Changing angles of attack and countering on both horizontal and vertical planes by slipping around the assailant's moves allows the defender to momentarily disappear from the attacker's line of sight, thereby facilitating an easier job of retaliating with a counterattack to end the fight and permit an escape to safety.

Of course, in a warrior tradition as comprehensive and far ranging in scope as ninjutsu, evasive tactics are not the only method taught to students. There are ninja *taijutsu* (unarmed combat) applications that rely on earth-like ground holding stability, water-like defensive backpeddling and angular counters, and fire-like forward moving stability, water-like defensive backpedaling evasion methods described here. The important point to emphasize, however, is the appropriateness of the response; these options are by no means arbitrary, and are determined by the type of attack confronted. In the case of an attacker who is stronger, faster, or possibly more skilled, the wind-like *fu no kata* tactics can best allow the ninja to overcome superior strength and speed to beat the technically "better" fighter.

C

The defender allows the attacker's low punch to slip by its intended target with a simple rocking back of the hips. The defender then captures the attacker's forward momentum and traps his punching arm with his torso and forearm. Forward leaning motion creates an arm bar along with an elbow slam to the side of the attacker's head. The defender can then hold the attacker in place with the barred elbow, freeing the defender's hands to do whatever is necessary.

A

D

B

E

The defender slips to his left to allow the attacker's leading hand speed punch to pass by. The defender's move is not a mere duck or flinch; he allows his knees to flex in order to avoid the direct hit. As he moves to the inside of the punch, the defender snaps his entire right arm up with a clubbing attack to the elbow joint of the punching arm. The attacker immediately attempts a rear hand punch, which is avoided with the same kind of shift. The defender then disappears from the attacker's view while applying a simultaneous palm-heel slam to the jaw and right knee takedown leverage to the attacker's right knee.

A

D

B

E

C

F

The defender evades an attacker's grab and punch attempt by leaving his hand right where it is held and slipping back around to the outside of the attacker's grabbing arm, using his body pivot and angling to free his hand from the attacker's grasp. The defender then uses his knee to pin the attacker in place for an elbow slam and finger twist takedown.

The attacker advances with an overhead club and swings at the defender's temple. Rather than attempt to stop the force of the larger assailant's blow, the defender shifts forward and to the outside of the club swing, allowing the weapon to pass harmlessly behind her. As a part of her forward motion, she projects her momentum so that her moving hips slam into the attacker's thigh and knock him to the ground. The defender's weight effortlessly breaks the attacker's leg, or at least slams him to the ground, so that she can quickly escape further attack attempts.

A

D

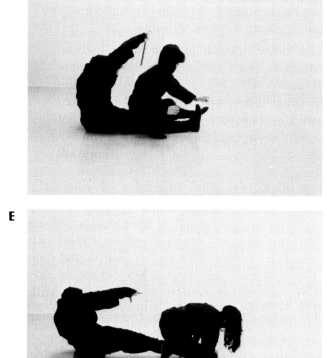

B

E

C

F

As the attacker swings his club with a horizontal smash to the shoulder, the defender tilts and moves forward inside the radius of the attacker's swing, allowing his thigh to hit the attacker's groin, his shoulder to slam into the attacker's upper ribs, and the side of his head to drive the attacker's head back. As the attacker falls back from the defender's stunning counterattack, the defender is able to lock the attacker's arm in an *onikudaki* shoulder dislocating leverage and wrench him to the ground.

A

D

B

E

C

The defender evades the attacker's punch with a crouch, and then springs back with a headbutt and forearm strike to knock the attacker's arm away. The defender then quickly sweeps the attacker's foot out from beneath him and then crushes his shin with a stamping kick.

A

B

C

D

E

F

To escape from the attacker's rear bearhug, the defender snaps his head and hips back to apply a double strike to the attacker's face and groin. The defender then grabs the backs of the attacker's hands, slips to one side to bind the attacker's arms against one another, and throws him over onto his back.

A

B

C

D

G

E

H

F

I

The defender slips to the inside of her attacker's karate-style, high round kick by stepping straight in toward the attacker's midsection with her own punch. From there, an arm hook throw from beneath the attacker's knee dumps him on the ground.

A

B

C

D

E

F

In another wind-like response against a kick, the defender slips to the outside of the moving leg. From his position of safety, the defender executes his own counter kick up into the underside of the attacker's outstretched leg to lift him up and dump him on his back. The defender can then follow up with a second kick against the downed attacker.

In response to a grab-and-punch situation, the defender counters with his own punch and then goes on to wrap his captured arm up and then under the attacker's grabbing arm. From that position, a body shift backwards pulls the attacker onto the ground or dislocates his shoulder.

A

B

C

D

G

E

H

F

I

D

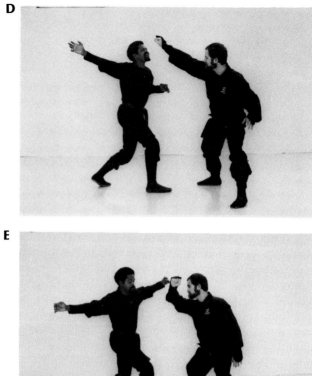

The defender uses two forearm smashes to knock away the attacker's two attempts at punching. Note that the body propels the forearms into their targets; it is not a matter of merely swinging the arms. A headbutt smash to the attacker's face is then followed by a forward hip throw that slings the dazed attacker onto the ground.

A

E

B

F

C

Wind-like taijutsu evasive action can also be used to counter a weapon attack as well. The defender slips to the outside of the attacker's sword thrust and captures the moving weapon. The defender then uses his foot to force the blade down and around into a new target. A forward body movement with the knees pushes the sword into the attacker.

E

G

F

H

3
NINJA ARUKI
THE STEALTHY TREAD OF THE NINJA

Much has been written, in historical as well as contemporary accounts of the ninja of Japan, concerning the *shinobi* warriors' legendary skill at moving undetected in and out of restricted or difficult areas by employing a knowledge of stealth and silent movement techniques. Methods of soundless walking, climbing, running, swimming, and leaping are known to be a part of the trained ninja warrior's arsenal of tools for accomplishment.

What many would-be students of the art of ninjutsu do not realize, however, is the fact that stealth methods cannot be taught as techniques in and of themselves, but rather must be cultivated through continued personal familiarization and bodily internalization. Just as the fist and foot examples of taijutsu unarmed fighting are not the art, but are instead merely training guides that can lead to the eventual perfection of the personal art of movement in combat scenarios, the stealth-walking methods are likewise only descriptions and not the ultimate answers themselves. Memorizing ways of technically placing the feet do not create an ability to move silently. Developing true grace and precision of movement is the only way to cultivate demonstrable skill.

NOISE

The way to begin stealth training is to explore first the nature of what creates noise or attracts attention. Take the time to watch yourself as you and others around you move through daily life. Be aware of all the normally unnoticed, unconsciously awkward actions, like doors being opened and closed with too much force, heels banging or sliding as feet move up and down stairways and along hallways in unthinking clumsiness, keys and books and tools being dropped or flung ungracefully to clatter noisily to rest, and human bodies overdoing routine movement actions through carefree lack of attention to detail. Once you have learned to observe the crude ungainliness that passes for normal motor habits, you will quickly begin to see that the first step toward successful silent movement skills is to simply eliminate all the unnecessary aspects of normal body motor actions.

Next on the list for self-training exercises for the development of stealth movement skill is to select examples of those places in which you feel that you might require the ability to move in silence, and practice normal movement in those environments. At first, it is recommended that you explore potential pitfalls by exaggerating normal movements to purposely create noise. That way, you have a clearer idea of exactly what needs to be eliminated. Once you have gotten into the spirit of tramping, shuffling, or crunching along in total disregard for potential noise, gradually begin paring away the unnecessary movement aspects that create the unwanted noise. Continued training with an ear toward detail will eventually gain you the natural grace you seek.

Guidelines for Stealth Walking

As an aid in assisting you to develop personal skills of silent movement for stalking, reconnaissance, or evasion, the following general guidelines will prove to be helpful:

1. Maintain balance control by allowing your body weight to sink and be carried on deeply flexed knees.
2. Remember to breathe along with your movement. Unconsciously holding your breath can unknowingly produce unneeded muscle tension, and could result in a gasping release of breath if you are startled or accidentally unbalanced.
3. Stay alert to the entire scene. Do not become so engrossed in watching your feet that you do not notice other people and elements entering the surroundings.
4. Use all your joints for movement, emphasizing fluidity through the engagement of the ankles, knees, and hips for stepping. Avoid the lazy and dangerous habit of stiffening the knees and swinging the entire leg from the hip.
5. Maintain your weight and balance on your grounded leg while you move the other leg into position to bear the weight. When absolute silence is a must, avoid distributing your weight over both legs at the same time.
6. If practical, allow your hands to float lightly in front of and beside your torso, one arm higher and one arm lower, to detect possible obstructions before your committed body weight encounters them.
7. Pause and hold your position if you feel that you have accidentally caused too much noise. Listen for signs that you were heard, such as the movements of others or the immediate silencing of background noise following your slip. Sink a little lower on your knees to physically relax the tension that could normally jump into your body with alarm. Take a deep breath and release it slowly to relax further. Continue your pause for as long as you feel it necessary to regain composure and allow possible listeners to decide that they did not hear anything after all.
8. Be as patient as possible. If speed of travel is not crucial, take as much time as you can. Impatience and the resultant hasty movement that it encourages are the greatest dangers to the person who must move silently without detection.
9. Keep your movement appropriate for the surroundings. Do not go to greater lengths than necessary to conceal your movement, while at the same time being aware of what others entering the area might see if they cannot hear. Total silence may not be needed when moving through wooded or densely populated areas where scattered noise is a natural part of the environment. Also bear in mind that low profile crawling or sliding may be the only way to move silently without being seen in some locations.

It must be emphasized that beyond a few technical tricks that could be taught to save the student a little time in the task of self-exploration, there is no special or magical technique that, once taught, will permit silent movement whenever needed. Skill is personal, and develops through experience by training as much as possible whenever possible. No quickly learned trick can replace reliable skill when it comes to the high-pressure realities of life-and-death survival situations.

The stealth movement examples on the following pages are provided as guidelines for training only. Once the student gains an idea of what to look for in practice, then begins the endless process of training for ever increasing proficiency. It should also be remembered that there are no set numbers of ninjutsu walking methods, nor are there any rigid or set forms that must be maintained. You will use your feet and body to move to where you have to be in the most efficient manner possible. Do not limit your training to the few sample methods that can appear in the limited space of this text. You are encouraged to explore, create, and fit your training discoveries to your personal needs.

The sweeping step of the ninja's stealth walking method allows your body weight to move in a steady and therefore silent manner over flooring that could prove to be difficult to negotiate quietly. This walking method is especially appropriate when crossing over wooden floors that could creak as the weight is shifted, or over ground that could produce unseen obstacles in the dark.

One leg holds the body weight while the other leg reaches out and gently explores the area where this new ground support leg will touch down. The probing foot comes up from behind the ground leg, passes through the center of balance near the ground leg ankle, and reaches out in front to check for possible objects in your way. (**Text and photos continue on page 34.**)

If there is no obstruction, the forward foot is eased onto the floor toes first. At the first signal of a creak or snap from the flooring, your foot can be pulled back to center and then reextended to a slightly different location. If there is no obstruction or sound, the body weight is gently shifted to the toes, outer edge, and then heel of this new ground foot, and what is now the rear foot becomes the new probing limb.

If it is necessary to turn and change directions, the probing leg is placed on the flooring already pointing in the new direction to be traveled. In that manner, your foot never needs to slide or turn on the floor surface where it could produce noise.

When first beginning training in this stepping fashion, care should be taken to move with patience and slowness, and to remember that balance comes from holding the knees in a deeply flexed position. Your body weight is held entirely over one single leg during all movement, except during those brief moments whent the weight moves on to the new supporting leg.

F

G

H

Small, tight, rolling steps are used to negotiate loose rock and dirt surfaces. The feet are flexed from the bottom in imitation of a rocking chair rocker, and move in a rolling shuffle from the back edge of the heel, across the sole lengthwise, and off the toes. The knees are held close together so that the ankles barely brush by one another without touching as the rear foot briskly moves into position as the new forward foot.

Your body weight and balance are held low over deeply flexed knees during the rather quick rolling steps. Care should be taken to move the body forward with your back extending straight up over your hips. Avoid the temptation to allow the shoulders to pitch forward in a leaning position. With the proper balance held over lowered hips, the rolling ankle work compacts the small stones in a downward manner to reduce the likelihood of the scraping sounds produced by feet shoving the gravel elements sideways against themselves and the ground surface.

A

B

C

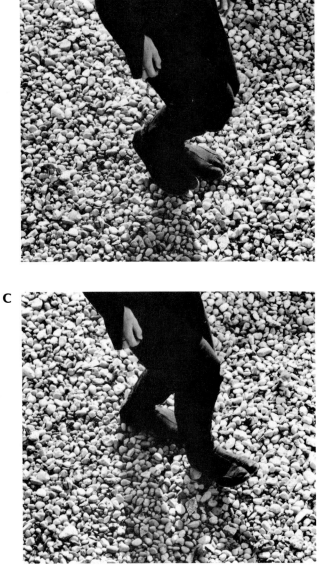

D

G

E

H

F

I

The turning step of the ninja stealth method is used in situations where continuous scanning is required during times of crossing open spaces that could expose you to detection by the enemy. As with almost all of the ninjutsu walking methods, it is crucial to keep your weight low and centered over deeply flexed knees in order to prevent loss of balance or awkward movement. The body moves as a total unit, the legs carrying the torso which supports and directs the scanning face. Avoid the danger of moving the body in such a way as to force the torso to twist against the hips or to require the head to turn on the neck independently of the body action. (**Text and photos continue on page 40**)

A   B   C

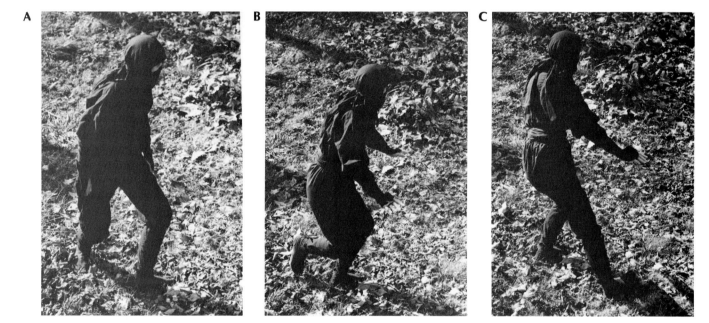

One foot maintains a ground position to support the body as the other foot ventures out to establish a new foothold. As this new ground foot is lowered into place, the ankle is turned and held in position to facilitate the alignment of the hips with the direction you are traveling. Place your foot on the ground already in line with where it should be when the previous ground leg is lifted up, so that there is no need to twist the foot on the ground surface in order to continue your body's turning progression.

J   K   L

The sweeping step is used to clear obstacles out of the path of progress. Your entire body weight and balance is held on the single ground leg and the forward leg reaches out with pointed toes to penetrate the reeds or grasses that stand in your way. Once the leg is extended forward, it is then moved to the side from your hip, creating a broad sweeping action that moves all obstructions to the side. In the case of grasses or tall weeds, the sideways folding action lays the plants down so that there is less sound generated when your foot comes to rest on top of the growth. Once the new forward foot is lowered into place, the body is shifted forward onto the new ground leg, allowing the rear leg to become the new probing limb.

C

A

B

D

E

From any of the ninjutsu stealth walking methods, it is possible to drop out of sight quickly whenever necessary. Should you feel that you might be spotted by a scout, illuminated by a searchlight, or hit by a projectile, you can use a direct body drop to the ground to disappear from the usual sight level. The body drop can be used to freeze yourself into immobility on the ground or can incorporate a follow-up rolling action to take you back onto your feet for escape or counter-attack action.

The *yokonagare* ("sideways flowing") body drop uses a sideways leaning drop to get you onto your seat as quickly as possible. Allow the reaching leg to act as a balancer to prevent you from toppling awkwardly, and keep the extended leg straight so that the bottom of the entire thigh absorbs the shock of the drop. Keep your eye on your adversary or the surroundings as you complete the roll that brings you back to your feet.

A

E

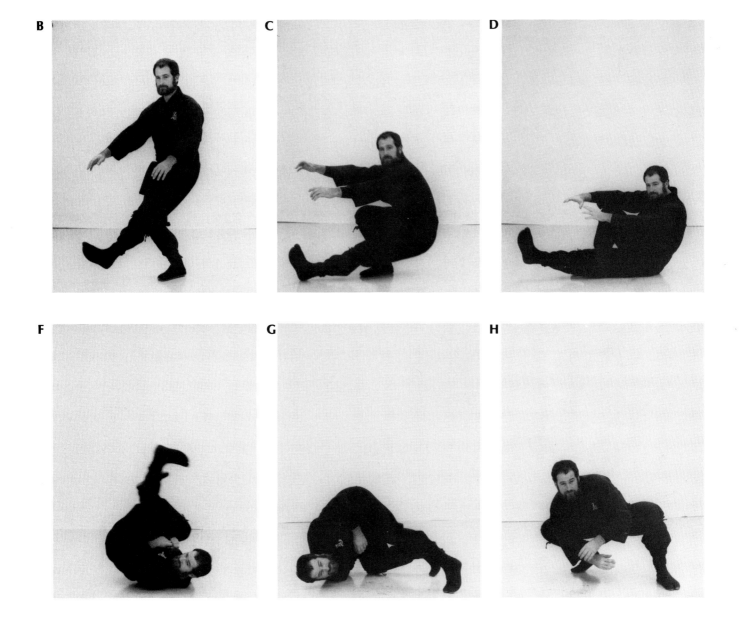

The *tachinagare* ("upright flowing") rear body drop takes you straight to your seat as you extend your leg forward as a balance facilitator and shock reducer. Impact with the ground is made with the entire bottom of the thigh, and the body is then tucked backward into a roll that brings you back to your feet again.

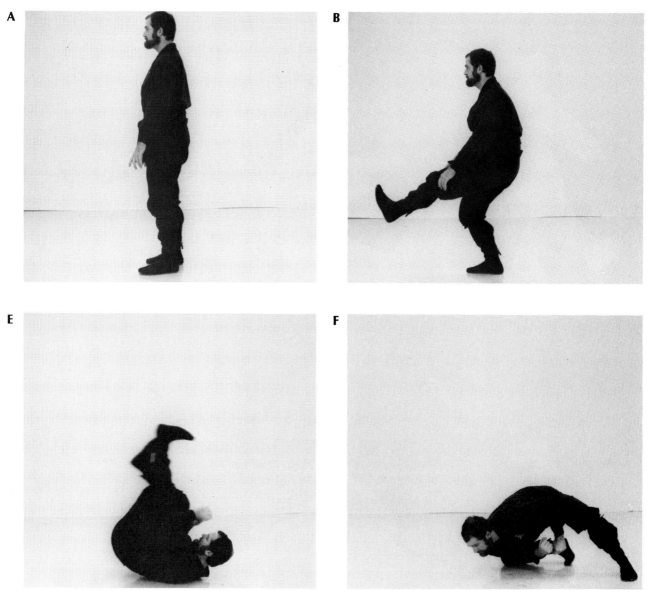

A

B

E

F

C

D

G

H

The *zenpo ukemi* ("forward breakfall") is used to drop straight forward to the ground. The entire bottom surfaces of both forearms are employed with a forward pushing/slapping action to break your fall. Avoid the dangerous tendency to reach out with your wrists or the palms of your hands only, just as you should avoid lifting your hands and hitting with your elbows only.

In this example, the drop begins from a kneeling position. Beginning students of the art usually find this technique easier to master than the full standing forward drop. Once confidence has been gained, you can move on to the more advanced version.

A

B

C

D

The full standing forward breakfall utilizes the entire forearm to absorb impact with the ground. As your body nears the ground surface, you can swing one leg up to reduce the jarring feel of hitting the ground. It is also advised that you be aware of the possibility of your face hitting the ground if your fall generates too much momentum. Turn your head to one side if necessary to protect your chin or face.

A

B

C

D

In more dangerous situations that require a lower profile, it could be necessary to drop to the ground and travel slowly on your hands and knees. Keep your face turning and scanning with every move, and coordinate your limb extensions with each inhalation and exhalation of your breathing cycle.

When moving, keep three of your limbs in a support position whenever you move the fourth limb to a new position. Place the stretch of your limbs so that the knee is advanced into the exact same spot on the ground that was occupied by the hand previously. That way there is a reduced likelihood of encountering any surprise sound-producing articles since the hand has previously cleared that spot. Avoid an up-and-down lurching motion to the body as you move along in a smooth flow of hand and leg actions.

A

D

G

When possible scanners could detect even the low posture of a hands-and-knees crawl, it may be necessary for you to adopt a flattened creeping body motion that uses the forearms and toes for forward motion. From a prone position, extend your arms forward and place your forearms flat against the ground surface, with the palms of your hands open and facing down. With your knees held straight, pull your toes as far forward as possible and wedge them against the ground surface. Tense your body from the center of your trunk outward and then use the momentary tension to lift your body up off the ground and pull yourself forward. Gently lower yourself to the ground again, and repeat the process. Remember to coordinate your breathing with your action; breathe in while setting up the move and breathe out while tensing and lifting the body.

A

B

E

4
NIN GU
NINJA TOOLS

The art of ninjutsu, or *nin-po* as it is often referred to in its higher and more spiritual order, is a system of total pragmatic self-protection for all circumstances and levels of human activity. The authentic historical methods were developed over the centuries in Japan, and reflect a keen awareness of all aspects of the environment that could, in any way, affect the potential outcome of a conflict for survival. Therefore, the tradition of ninjutsu is to apply state-of-the-art thinking and tools, under the guidance of enlightened awareness and skill in embodying and manifesting certain universal principles, to accomplish one's goals.

The historical lore of Japanese ninjutsu is full of references to a broad array of ingenious, multipurpose tools developed by the original ninja families of the Iga and Koga regions during the feudal age. Such antique tools as the *kusari-gama* chain and sickle, *tetsubishi* caltrop spikes, *taruikada* foot flotation pots, *tsubogiri* wall borers, and *gando* candle spotlights are fascinating to modern practitioners of ninjutsu, more for their reference to the creativity of our spiritual ancestors than as usable tools in contemporary society. In the museum pieces, we can see reflected the original ninja families' responses to the architecture, dress, technology and terrain of their day.

In those same museum displays, we can also find the inspiration for the adaptation of the same universal principles in our contemporary environment. The ninja of today no longer needs to train with *sodezutsu* single-shot wooden-hand-held cannons, now that the world has modern light weight rapid-fire handguns. The ancient ninja's ingenious bamboo tube *uchidake* firestarter has been replaced by the inexpensive disposable cigarette lighter. The *tsugibune* collapsible boat, though once state-of-the-art in clandestine water transportation, is now awkward and out of date when compared to today's inflatable rubber canoes and skiffs. *Igabakama* tight-ankled pantaloon tie-on leggings and cotton-soled split-toed tabi have given way to their buttoned, snapped, and zippered descendents, rendering the well-known *shinobi shozoku* (ninja costume) into a mere museum piece in the world of the twentieth century.

Though the details of technology evolve and grow with society, certain principles do seem to remain constant throughout all time, however. These key principles form the backbone of the ninja combat methods, and rely on concepts of movement and responsive interaction rather than set mechanical routines or applications for success. Therefore, today's students of *nin-po* can enjoy training with certain antique ninja tools in order to better understand the universal scope of the principles that can apply to all weapon/tools regardless of the age. The *kyoketsu shoge* ringed-cord-and-dagger skills are also models for persons who might have to defend themselves with mountain climbing gear, auto shop trouble light cables, or even the common telephone receiver on its cord. The historical *shuriken* throwing star can easily be replaced with coins from the pocket, coffee cup saucers, or shards of broken window glass. The *hanbo* half-staff today is a walking stick, a fireplace poker, or a child's softball bat.

In addition to providing pragmatic self-protection knowledge, the experience of historical weapon training can also provide a sense of the vast centuries-long tradition that lies in silent endorsement behind today's Bujinkan dojo warrior arts training halls. Without the generations of ancestors who gambled their lives in order to develop the methods that we are privileged to study today, this art would be nothing more than untried theory or a pointless system of violent recreation. To attempt to create a warrior arts training system without the experience of actually employing the methods taught while under the normal extreme duress of a life-and-death confrontation would be the height of fraud. No mere made-up martial art with self-appointed grandmasters, the authentic ninja warrior tradition is founded and based on the documented experiences of those families who went on to create a place for themselves in Japanese history.

In the teaching of the *shinobi* warrior's art, the word "tool" is preferred over the more common term "weapon." Tools are thought of as aids that enhance the normal mechanical motions of the human body in the pursuit of accomplishing necessary actions. On the other hand, weapons are immediately associated with damage to other persons or animals.

Though it may seem at first to be a small difference in language usage, the choice of the tool concept over the weapons concept is an important one in the ninjutsu training hall. In the first place, by concentrating on tools, the student is encouraged to view his or her actions as positive working movements rather than as destructive fighting techniques. The student comes to feel less of a potential thrill for violence that way. A second consideration is the fact that weapons are often seen as special things unto themselves, and the student can come to place too much reliance on always having a specific weapon at hand or in the pocket.

Tools for self-protection are always available to the practitioner who has come to view the whole world as his or her training hall. There is no need to always have a ninja *tanto* at hand when there are kitchen and garden knives, metal rulers, scissors, and screwdrivers around. The *kusari-fundo* weighted chain can be left in the dojo, as long as there are belts with buckles, cameras on straps, neckties, or shoulder purses around. And though mere possession of the Okinawan karate *nunchaku* could, in many communities, get the martial artist arrested without question, one is rarely suspected of plotting evil deeds just because he or she has effective weapons such as a child's baseball bat, a hand sickle, or rat-tailed comb nearby. A can of orange spray paint could be used to blind and mark an attacker.

When beginning a study of the tools that are a part of the traditional ninja's combat art, the student can at first discern five roughly defined groups:

- sticks
- blades
- flexibles
- projectiles
- combinations

For practical self-protection training, the best weapons for practice are those that closely match what will usually be close at hand at the time of an attack. Likewise, less emphasis will be placed on those weapon types not at all likely to be available during an attack. Citizens of countries or states where handguns, shuriken stars, or *kusarifundo* chains are illegal would be less in need of training in those weapons in their literal form. However, when viewed as general weapon types, there are limitless, totally legal devices that could easily be substituted for any of these historical ninjutsu weapon/tools. In this light, it can be seen that the art will never outgrow itself or become antiquated, as long as the tradition of adaptive thinking continues to be taught as an integral part of the ninja's life art.

THE NINJA *HANBO*

One of the most practical weapons throughout all ages of mankind, the stick or cane is easily kept at hand or can be found readily in one of many guises. Referred to as the *hanbo*, or "half staff" in

Japanese, this tool is one of the most reliable to be found in the ninja's arsenal. Although the humble *hanbo* lacks in glamour when compared with the samurai sword or battlefield halberd, it is a trusted friend to the warrior no matter what the land in which he finds himself.

The *hanbo* can be used for striking, throwing, or locking techniques, and when applied with appropriate body-angling methods, can allow the proficient fighter to move inside or outside of the danger in order to disarm his or her assailant readily.

Striking Methods

The *hanbo* cane can be gripped with both hands for strength and leverage, or with only one hand for speed and maneuverability. Both forward and reverse grips can be utilized with the *hanbo*, and a wide variety of footwork methods can be employed to take the cane to its target.

It is important to note that the *hanbo* cane itself is rarely if ever used to block the striking attack of an attacker. Blocking as such is a rather crude form of defense in that it requires too much time and energy commitment to an action that can too easily leave the stick holder open to an immediate follow-up attack. It is far more economical and efficient to use the cane to stun or damage the limbs of the attacker as he advances, rather than merely cover up against his onslaught. Through effective taijutsu body movement and positioning, the skillful stick fighter allows the attacker's weapon to move harmlessly by while he or she launches a counterattack from the safety of a strategic position.

As with the taijutsu unarmed counterparts, the striking techniques of the ninja's cane fighting employ the full body weight behind the strike for knockdown power. In this example of *jodan uchi* high-level strike, the ankles and knees carry the strike to the target.

A

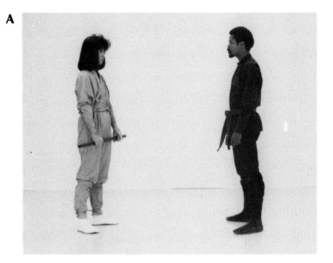

B

C

Chudan uchi middle-level hanbo strike   *Gedan uchi* lower-target hanbo strike

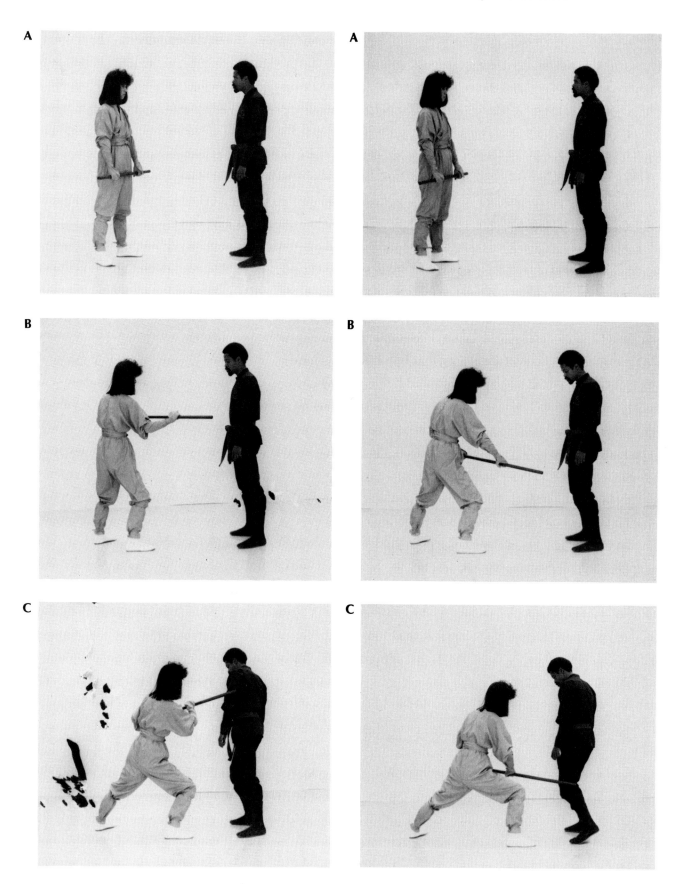

Against a high punching attack, the defender can
slide back and to the inside of the attacker's moving
arm where he is out of reach. From the safety of his
distant position, the defender is in a perfect spot to
swing his cane back into the forward-moving ribs of
the attacker. By rocking forward on his knees with the
impact, the defender can intensify the stopping
power of the blow.

With back-pedaling footwork similar to that of the previous example, the defender can move back and to the outside of the attacking arm with a cane tip slam to the ribs. Again, the defender makes no attempt to block the quickly moving limb. Instead, he allows the arm to move by unhindered so that the attacker's body actually supplies the stopping power of the impact with the cane tip.

A

B

C

D

Again from the waiting *katayaburi no kamae* posture, the defender slips past the attacker's punch, this time with aggressive rather than defensive footwork, to counterstrike with the moving end of his cane. Once his momentum has been stopped by the attacker's advance, the defender steps back with his rear foot and swings around to throw the attacker on the ground. By using proper timing and leverage, the defender can knock his attacker down without having to rely on bone and muscle power alone.

D

A

E

B

F

C

G

From the *munenmuso no kamae* posture, the defender observes as the attacker advances with a lunging punch. As the punch approaches, the defender matches the timing with a rearward drift and a rising cane strike to the attacker's punching arm. As soon as the arm has been knocked away, the defender rocks back in with a smash to the attacker's head. A two-handed grip on the stick increases the defender's leverage.

A

B

C

D

E

F

Against a kick, the defender allows his footwork to take him inside the reach of the moving leg, where he is then in a good position to counterattack with a cane tip to the throat. Again, the attacker's body momentum provides the power for the blow that stuns him. The defender then finishes off the attacker with a powerful two-handed cane slam to the head.

A

B

C

E

F

G

Hanbo Grappling

Just as the *hanbo* striking methods mirror the *nin-po* taijutsu unarmed *koppojutsu* (bone-damaging methods) and *koshijutsu* (muscle- and organ-damaging methods) tactics and applications, the *hanbo*-grappling methods are models of the unarmed *jutaijutsu* grappling applications. The thorough student of the warrior arts will want to cover all possibilities in training, and the possibility of having a weapon seized or taken away and used against oneself is certainly within the realm of the probable that must be prepared for.

When working with ninja methods for weapon retention or with disarmament methods, it is important to remember that the esssence of taijutsu body action is the flowing delivery of body movements that coordinate the use of all four limbs with the torso and the breath. The most serious mistake that a student can make when practicing weapon-disarm tactics is to freeze the body in position and attempt to rely on the strength of the arms alone for results. By engaging the body trunk for angling to take away the attacker's power, and using the flexing of the legs for rising and lowering to throw the attacker off balance, the practitioner of ninjutsu learns to effectively and efficiently gain control of the confrontation.

In this example of the hanbo cane in use as a grappling tool against a punching attacker, the defender angles back and away from the incoming punch to apply a simultaneous rear-handed cane strike to the ribs and leading hand punch to the attacking forearm. The defender then grabs the punching arm and uses her cane for leverage to throw the attacker to the floor face-down.

A

D

E

Against a punching advance, the defender slips by the attacker's moving fist to bring the leading tip of her cane down hard against his elbow. From that position, she uses her body weight in motion to drive her leading arm wrist into the attacker's throat. She leaves her cane in place and moves behind the attacker where he cannot get at her easily. From her position behind the attacker, the defender reaches across to secure a grip on the leading end of the cane, which is then used to facilitate a neck-snapping choke and takedown.

A

D

G

B

C

E

F

H

I

Against an attacker's attempt to grab the defender's wrist and punch him, the defender steps back and uses sinking body leverage to force the cane down on the top of the attacker's wrist as a means of driving him to the ground. In an actual assault scenario, the entire sequence should be performed as one continuous flow of movements.

A

D

In another variation of the ninja stick grappling art used against a grab-and-punch attempt, the defender uses his foot to propel the cane into the attacker's groin, since the defender's hand is held immobilized on the cane. Following the strike, the defender shifts back and away from a possible punch, and in so doing, topples the attacker with his cane leverage against the insides of the thighs. If the downed attacker attempts to kick from the ground, the defender can swat the shin of his moving leg with his cane.

A

B

E

F

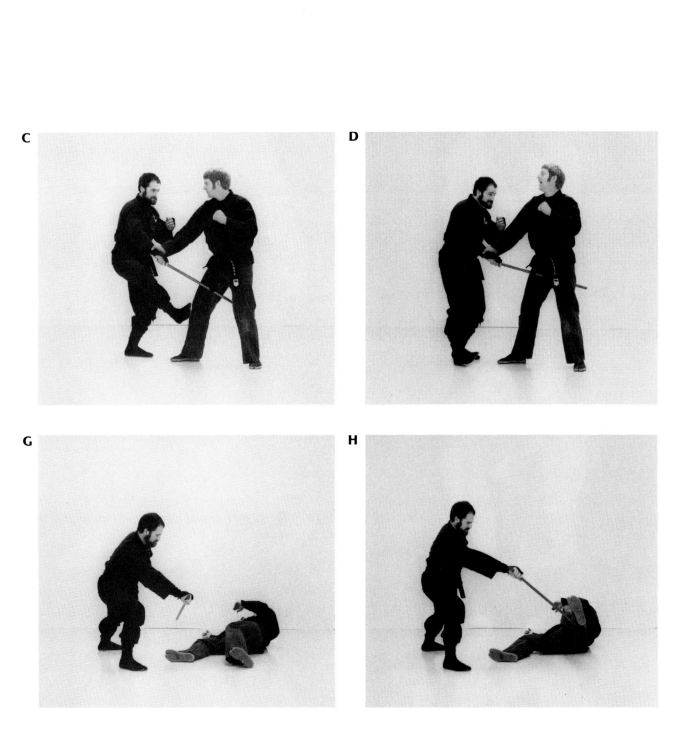

The defender leaves his immobilized arm in place and pulls his cane away from an attacker's attempt at a grasp. Continuing his pulling motion away from the attacker, the defender uses his hanbo to trap the defender's hand. The bones in the back of the attacker's grabbing hand are crushed between the cane and the defender's wrist. The defender then uses his body weight in motion to swing the cane tip into position to pull the attacker down with throat-crushing pressure from the cane.

A

B

C

D

E

F

The more simple the action, the more likely that the desired results will be produced. In this example, the defender ignores the grab for a moment and attacks his assailant's foot with a downward stab. The defender then pins the startled attacker's foot in place with his own and uses leaning pressure from his cane to topple the attacker. Because the attacker's foot is held firmly in place flat on the ground, his falling body momentum works to break his own ankle.

A

B

C

D

E

F

Against a sleeve grab, the defender raises his cane to strike the attacker in the face. The attacker quickly grabs the cane, however, and attempts to overpower the defender. Rather than wrestle and struggle to free his cane, the defender allows the attacker to maintain his grip and uses backward circling footwork to sling the attacker onto the ground.

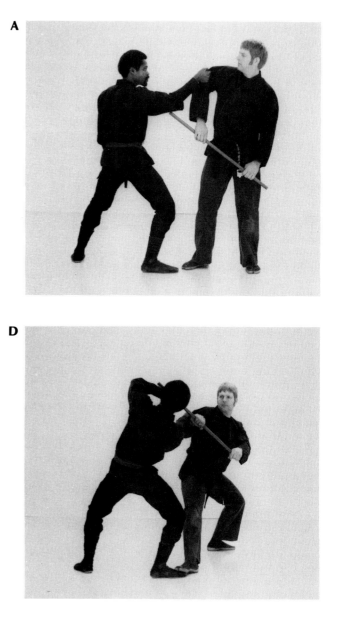

B

C

E

F

The defender backs up and slams his cane up into the undersides of the attacker's forearms to loosen his grip. He then immediately launches into a forward slam to the attacker's ribs to knock him back. The defender crosses his hanbo from beneath the attacker's outstretched arms to prevent him from escaping, and then uses rocking body motion to throw the attacker onto the ground.

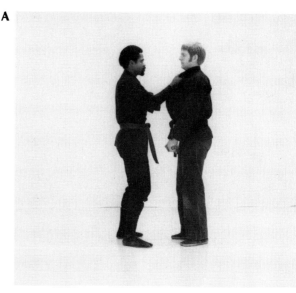

A

D

G

B

C

E

F

H

I

THE NINJA SWORD

Along with the spear and bow and arrow, the sword was considered to be one of the three principal weapons of feudal Japan. Any warrior desiring to survive through a full lifetime was sure to be a master of sword technique. Because of the ninja's need to be able to move through tight spaces and disappear into the shadows when necessary, his sword was often a shorter blade than his samurai adversary's battlefield length *tachi*. Though a graceful curve to the blade was preferred, it was often impossible for the historical ninja to obtain such a work of art. His sword was occasionally a rather straight *chokuto*-style blade.

Contrary to what is constantly portrayed in ninja stories on television and the movie screen, the skilled swordsman avoided at all costs slamming the cutting edge of his sword into the edge of his adversary's sword. The enemy's blade is to be avoided through positioning, not blocked, and the fight taken to the enemy in a direct manner. Just like the ninja's unarmed combat method, the kenjutsu of *nin-po* utilizes effective movement of the body out of the incoming weapon's path, coupled with strategic placement of one's own weapon for an unhindered counterattack as general guidelines for training toward life-or-death combat efficiency.

Gripping the Sword

Traditionally, the two-handed grip was used to give the Japanese sword better leverage for cutting, and a more responsive feel for angling. The right hand always grips the handle just below the *tsuba* handguard, allowing enough distance from the guard so that the thumb and pointer finger do not rub against the metal *tsuba*. The handguard itself actually serves more to guard the sword-bearer from the possibility of his hand slipping down along the cutting edge of the blade in the heat of bloody battle than it does as a protective barrier behind which to hide from the adversary's blade. Therefore, it is not necessary to position the right hand close and tight beneath the *tsuba*. The left hand grips the handle at its base, so that there is a gap between the two hands when they are in fighting position.

When properly gripped, the swordhandle should lie diagonally along both palms of the hands. This allows the blade's cutting edge and point to reach out for its target in a natural way when the arms are extended. The incorrect "sledgehammer" grip, where the handle lies at right angles to the bones of the hands, requires awkward wrist bending in order to execute cutting techniques.

The sword is gripped firmly with the lower two or three fingers of each hand, leaving the upper fingers and thumb free for their influence in subtle blade angling as the sword moves toward its target

Properly gripped, the sword handle lies diagonally across the palms with the lower three fingers of each hand holding the tool in position. Be sure to leave a sufficient gap between the handguard and the right hand, as well as between the upper right and lower left gripping hands.

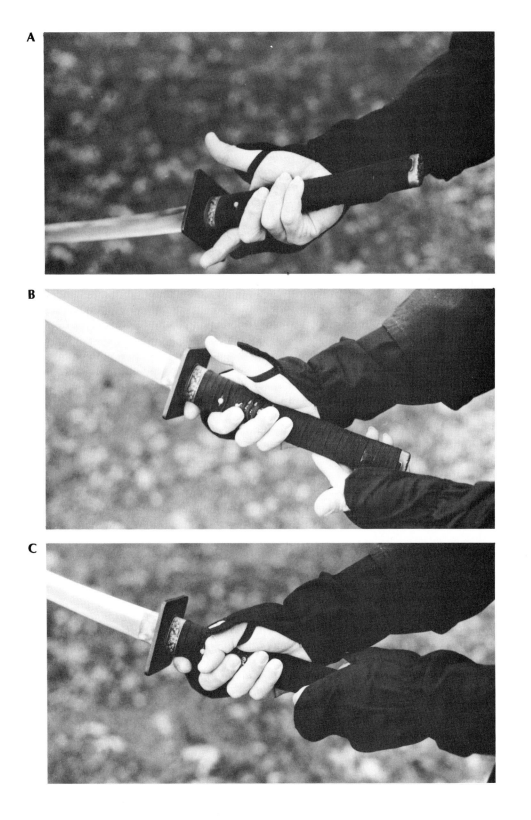

Fighting Postures

In the *kenjutsu* sword combat method of the ninja, the body, mind, and sword of the fighter act as a single unit to embody and give life to the intention. Therefore, as one prepares to move against an enemy with a cut, the body must reflect the intentions and attitudes of the sword-bearer. In the *nin-po* combat method, these physical embodiments of inner feelings are referred to as *kamae*, or "attitudes," rather than as the more static sounding "stances."

From each *kamae* positioning of the body, sword, and mind, certain cuts proceed naturally. Each posture is in effect a temporary staging point from which cutting actions are launched.

Kongo no kamae.

Kocho no kamae.

Jizurigedan no kamae.

Daijodan no kamae.

Hasso no kamae.

Ichi no kamae.

Seigan no kamae.

Gedan no kamae.

Ryusui no kamae.

Cutting

The essence of the ninjutsu sword method is in cutting down the enemy with as little risk, time, energy, and complexity as possible. Though many readers may at first think that the foregoing statement is so obvious a truth that it does not need to be included in this work, it is important to point out that few sword teachers in the world today teach anything to do with actual combat, and there is much behind the obvious that rarely surfaces in the conventional training hall.

Cutting with the Japanese sword involves a carefully coordinated blending of body motion, limb extension, descending blade dynamics, and cutting edge slicing. Far more refined and therefore more difficult than a woodsman's ax chopping motion, the proper and effective sword cut takes thousands of hours of repetitive work to perfect. The most effective cut descends to its target with a pushing slide along the forward one-third of the blade, with the swordsman's whole body moving in perfect coordination behind the cut to provide smooth fluid power. Cutting actions that engage the limbs alone for power or maneuverability are to be avoided, as are pulling cuts that cause the wounded enemy to fly forward into the startled swordbearer as the blade catches and pulls the enemy's flesh or bone structure.

The Japanese sword draw is a blending of two actions; the sword is cleared from its scabbard for combat and makes its first cut all in the same motion. Note that the blade is not merely pulled from a stationary scabbard. The handle is propelled forward with the drawing right hand while the scabbard is pulled back to clear the end of the blade with the retreating left hand. In order to provide cutting power to penetrate the target, the body rocks forward over the legs as a part of the draw.

A

C

B

D

E

From the front, it is possible to see that the sword leaves its scabbard in a direct line; it is not lifted out and then lowered for cutting action. In this example, the swordsman immediately follows up with a downward cut and thrusting stab to finish the technique.

To replace the sword in its *saiya*, the spine edge of
the blade is pulled across the scabbard opening to
align the point for insertion. The scabbard is pushed
up over the blade as the blade is lowered. The
resheathed sword is then once again positioned on
the hip.

C

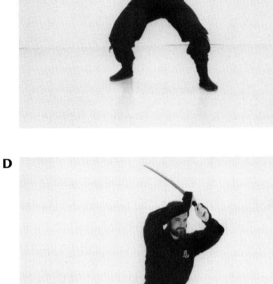

To perform the lunging vertical cut, the feet move briskly forward as the sword is raised to a 45-degree-angle *daijodan no kamae* over your head and then sent down and forward. The entire action is performed as a flow without interruption or pause in the rising and lowering of the sword. For the most efficient cutting action, do not allow the blade to rise any higher than the 45-degree-angle position.

A

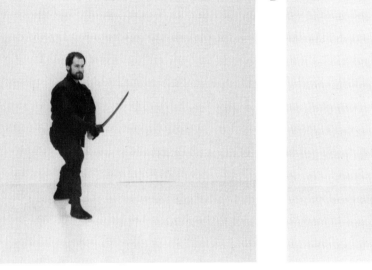

D

B

E

From the *hasso* posture, the blade is leveled out to cut through the target in a horizontal path. Be sure to allow your breathing action to mirror the cycles of muscular relaxation and contraction that go through your body as you push the cutting edge through its target.

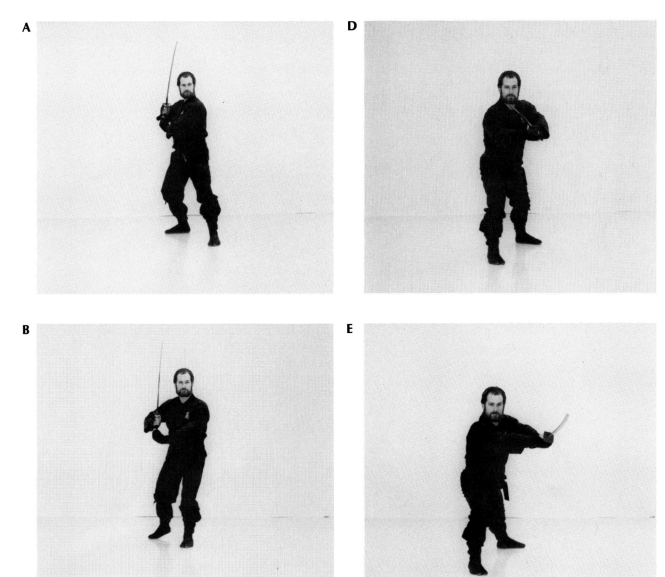

A piercing thrust can be executed from the *seigan no kamae* by rocking forward on the knees to send the hips and torso forward. The arms and sword are propelled by the forward body motion, and do not move as separate units by themselves.

A

B

C

By throwing the rear foot forward and to the side, the body and arms move in harmony to project the twisting blade into its target. When properly executed, the tip of the blade locks on its target and seems to pull the arms behind it as it flies forward from the *kocho no kamae*.

From a waiting *kongo no kamae* posture, the defender defies the attacker to make his move. As the attacker flies forward with a vertical cut, the defender allows his body to tip to one side as he lowers and then pushes through with his sword blade. The hapless attacker ends up cutting his own wrist, arm, and neck as his body momentum carries him along the edge of the defender's sword.

A

D

B

E

C

The defending swordsman uses body angling and turning to avoid the attacker's sword and drive the cutting edge of his own blade into the attacker's chest to cut him open and knock him down. Proper body positioning on deeply flexed knees is one of the keys to making this technique work effectively.

A

B

C

D

E

F

The attacker advances with a sideward smack from his sword in order to clear the defender's blade out of the way for a thrust to the midsection. Rather than resist the pressure on the side of his sword, however, the defender allows himself to be pushed out of the way entirely so that his footwork takes him out at an angle to the stabbing attempt. From this new angle, it is easy to allow the tip of his sword to slide up and across the back of the attacker's advancing wrist. An additional push into the attacker's arm helps to end the fight.

A

B

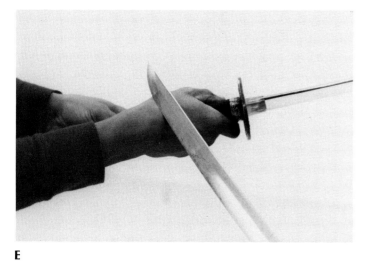

E

F

C

D

G

A

In another method of dealing with an attacking swordsman's thrust, the defender uses a circular smacking action from his low *gedan no kamae* pose to redirect the advancing blade. From the defender's viewpoint the locked blades are seen to go around in a clockwise direction, passing in front of the attacker's forward leg to cut it as the defender clears his forward leg. At the top of the circular swing, the defender suddenly drops his blade down on the attacker's forearms and uses his body weight to shove the cut across the two targets. A sudden reversal lifts the blade to catch the attacker across the throat and knock him backward to the ground.

D

E

H

I

B

C

F

G

J

K

The drawing cut slices through the attacker's midsection as the defender moves to the outside of the attacker's descending blade. A two-handed grip piercing thrust to the ribs follows the cut to force the attacker back.

A

B

E

C

D

F

G

The defending swordsman uses a rather unconventional backhanded reverse grip to pull the sword from its scabbard and cut the attacker as the attacker attempts a horizontal cut to the defender's neck. Note the crucial use of the body movement to clear the attacker's blade and drive the defending blade back across the attacker's outstretched arms.

A

D

B

C

E

F

5
IN-TON
CONCEALMENT AND CAMOUFLAGE FOR THE NINJA

Perhaps one of the most efficient means of self-protection is simply to not be seen or noticed at all, thereby removing the possibility of becoming a target, a victim, or a person forced to be involved in a conflict requiring self-defense. Any confrontation has the possibility of becoming a dangerous situation; court records are filled with stories of traffic congestion rudeness that erupted into brutal fistfights, and of arguments among friends that escalated into fatal shootings or stabbings. In times of war or revolution, the considerations are even more urgent. The unnecessary expenditure of costly or scarce supplies and the sacrificing of the lives of loved ones can be reduced greatly by avoiding the conventional battlefield altogether. It is difficult for the oppressor or attacker to defeat an enemy that he cannot perceive. This finely developed art of invisibility is one of the principal methods employed by the ninja warriors of Japan.

PERSPECTIVES ON THE ART OF INVISIBILITY

The power of invisibility can be developed on the physical level. Many of the concepts of invisibility embodied in the strategies of espionage and commando tactics for which the historical ninja were famous came to Japan with the hoards of Chinese military and religious authorities fleeing the devastation following the fall of the T'ang dynasty.

Often quoted as another source for some of the warfare strategies of ninjutsu, the classical Chinese treatise on war compiled by *Sonshi* (*Sun Tzu* in Chinese) contains many references to the proper methods of clandestine operation and reconnaissance that had long been proven successful in China. *Sun Tzu's Art of War* is said to have been introduced to Japan in the middle years of the eighth century by the traveling Japanese scholar *Kibi no Makibi*. The thirteenth and final chapter of the work deals with the use of spies and espionage, and though rejected with contempt and disgust by many of the more conventional warlords of pre-feudal Japan, the teachings were well received and taken to heart by the vastly outnumbered families who dwelled in the mountains of the Iga and Koga regions.

The power of invisibility can also be developed on the mental or psychological level. Like the Japanese art of ninjutsu, the highly secret Tibetan warrior tradition of *trulkor* is based largely on the creation of images. Translated literally as "illusion action," the esoteric doctrine which mirrors the methods of Japan's ninja stipulates that all combat is based on deception. By creating shapes and images to confuse and delude the adversary, the skilled warrior conceals his true capabilities and intentions. His first target is the mind of his adversary. From that point he goes on to secure the total victory. Like his Tibetan *trulkor* counterparts, the ninja moves like a ghost in the moonlight, unseen, unheard, and unnoticed, while the enemy takes to the battlefields all exposed, vulnerable, and fearful, never knowing just where or how its nemesis will appear.

The power of invisibility can be developed through spiritual perfection. Strongly influencing the development of the *shugendo* and *mikkyo* spiritual traditions that contributed to the body of knowlege studied by the historical ninja of Japan, the *vedas* and *sutras* of the Himalayan cultures contain numerous references to the development of reliable psychic skills for personal self-protection. Ultimately the real roots of the ninja's power methods do not lie in China as many historians assert, but past the Himalaya Mountains along the ancient Silk Road.

The yoga *sutras* of Patanjali tell of the powers that can be developed through the practice of *samyama*, or the three-part inspired blending of intense concentration, meditative flow, and the complete absorbing/merging of the consciousness with the object of concentration. The resulting *siddhis*, or "accomplishments," sound like a literal description of the legendary abilities of the ninja warriors of the night.

Applying samyama *on the physical form of one's body obstructs its perceptibility and removes the ability of others to see the body. The light emanating from the body does not register in the eyes of the beholder, rendering one invisible.*

From this procedure also arises the ability to remove all sound and other physical sense aspects.

Applying samyama *to the inner light gives one intuitive knowledge of that which is subtle, concealed, or distant.*

Through the mastery of udana *meditative breathing, one gains the ability to levitate over obstacles and walk over water and swamps.*

Applying samyama *to the relationship between the physical body and the ether (substance that supports the subatomic particles), and to the floating quality of lightweight objects gives one the ability to fly through the air.*

Though spiritual methods of rendering the body invisible, as taught by enlightened mystics such as India's Patanjali, Togakure *shugendo's*

Gakumon Gyoja, or Iga *sennin* wizard Kain Doshi, are of inspiration to neophyte students as they look ahead at what future training can provide, the ninja's skills of invisibility begin with physical fundamentals of how to avoid being detected. Once an attitude of confidence in one's ability to move unperceived has been allowed to develop, the student of ninjutsu can then, with unhesitating spirit, move on to the higher, rarer levels of *onshinjutsu*, the art of making oneself invisible.

PHYSICAL METHODS OF BECOMING INVISIBLE

Darkness is one of the ninja's most formidable weapons. The simplest method of becoming invisible is to remove the ability of others to see you. In a totally darkened room, everything becomes invisible. Chairs, tables, stairwells, guard dogs, people—all become impossible to see when there is no light to be reflected back to the eyes of the perceiver. From the standpoint of the ninja's operational activity, darkness provides an excellent form of passive defense, in that most countermeasures and weapons require optical guidance to be effective. Without a target to sight in on, an attacker finds it difficult for blades, sticks, hands, even bullets, to be effective.

Camouflage

Further measures to lessen the likelihood of being seen include camouflage techniques for the individual warrior. Reduced conspicuousness can be attained by wearing garments appropriate to the area or the lighting in which the ninja will be operating. It should be noted that night camouflage entails much more than merely slipping into a black suit. Actually, an all-black uniform or color scheme is optimal only on certain occasions, because in any condition other than total darkness, black clothing tends to create an intense solid silhouette. Another negative consideration is the implication that all-black attire would have if spotted. Someone lurking about furtively in a black "secret agent" outfit of deck shoes and commando sweater, let alone a fifteenth-century ninja costume, is certain to be assumed as being up to no good if encountered by police or security personnel.

In urban or built-up areas, tones of gray, tan, or blue are best suited for image-concealing clothing. The ninja wearing a dark gray warm-up suit or a blue denim jacket-and-jeans combination can easily fade into the shadows when necessary, and will stand a better chance of moving unchallenged or at least explaining his or her way out if confronted. Running shoes, a rolled-up watch cap, a light sheen of perspiration, or even a towel or scarf around the neck or over the lower face will seem to be a natural part of the attire and should not create any additional suspicion at all.

Operations in wooded or field situations can be facilitated by wearing various tones of green or tan. Today's military preference for subdued shades of olive green, khaki, or camouflage pattern uniforms is easily adapted to ninjutsu training or work. The military colors blend readily with natural wooded or desert surroundings, and fade to dull grays in the reduced light of night.

Care must be taken to cover or camouflage the entire body. Natural body oils make the skin highly reflective, and a face can stick out like a beacon to an observer scanning a wooded or partially lighted area. When possible, tone down exposed skin areas with dirt, ashes, charcoal, shoe polish, or stick paint make-up. The historical ninja of Japan sometimes used specially constructed half-sleeves to cover the backs of their hands, and cloth strips to form a combination hood and mask to conceal the face and muffle the breathing.

Physical skills of invisibility are essential in cases where infiltration, exfiltration, insertion, or extraction are required to protect the lives of loved ones or those for whom we are responsible. As an all-around warrior, the ninja trains to be able to use nature as a combat ally whenever possible. Darkness, with its concealing qualities, is first friend to the *shinobi* warrior.

In addition to camouflage skills of concealing one's presence from view, the ninja's arts of invisibility also involve abilities of moving through hostile territory without being encountered by enemy personnel. In this example of gaining access to a building under the cover of concealment, the ninja moves up a steel staircase beneath the steps, rather than take a chance on being spotted in the more conspicuous topside position. (It should be noted that for reasons of presentation clarity the photographs were taken during daylight hours. In actual application, night's darkness would aid the climber in his need for invisibility.

A

D

G

In this example of Togakure ryu ninjutsu's *shoten no jutsu* "vertical surface running," the ninja climbs to the roof of a building by means of an elevated escape ladder that has been mounted in such a way as to prevent access by the average person. Never one to settle for the average, the ninja is able to use his skills and knowledge of balance, momentum, and timing to carry his body twice the distance of his height onto the ladder. Once he has a firm grip on the ladder, the ninja continues his ascent upward, being aware of staying flat against the climbing surface and of continually scanning his surroundings to check for others who might spot him.

A

D

E

B

C

F

G

In another example of clandestine movement, the ninja uses the angling of his body joints to facilitate silent access onto a rooftop as a means of escaping hostile pursuers. Though unenlightened critics of the *shinobi* arts are quick to claim that such skills are easily adapted to immoral purposes such as burglary or terrorism, in truth, the question of morality is outside of the reality of training one's body to operate efficiently at one's command. It is difficult to imagine any parent who would not want their child to have the ability to physically vanish from the path of brutal and animalistic pursuers chasing them, regardless of the fact that it could be possible for other persons in other places to misuse such evasive skills for immoral personal gain.

A

B

G

H

C

D

E

F

I

J

K

L

Ninjutsu covert climbing skills involve the scientific use of the body's mechanics and dynamics for efficient scaling. In this example, the climber uses outstretched limbs for movement, as opposed to tightly bent joints that tax and tire the muscles too quickly. Three points of contact are maintained at all times as the fourth limb is moved to seek out a new firm anchor. Breathing rhythm matches muscle contraction and relaxation. It is also important to be aware of keeping the body flat against the climbing surface at all times to avoid having to tense the muscles at awkward moments to prevent falling back. Wall hugging also produces a less-noticeable silhouette should a casual observer glance at the climber during the night.

B

D

There will be occasions when a suspended rope or chain may be the only access to escape into, or out of, a structure. Therefore, a scientific method of gripping the rope and moving the body up or down is a part of ninjutsu survival training. The rope is gripped at an angle across the palm of the hand, just as with a sword handle or hanbo cane. The body is held naturally upright for ease of movement and balance. The rope is allowed to wrap around the outside of the calf and across the top of one foot in order to afford gripping purchase with the bottom of the other foot. The feet hold while the arms extend and secure a higher grip on the rope. The hands then bear the load while the feet relax their grip to permit the legs to fold and move up the rope. Again the feet grab and hold the weight while the hands move up again. At any time during the ascent or descent, the feet can lock onto the rope to permit relatively free use of the hands, should something be needed from a pocket or pack.

A

C

B

D

E

G

F

H

Psychological Factors

With the proper frame of mind, the ninja moving through the night has a distinct psychological advantage over an adversary. Humans seem to fear the darkness instinctively, perhaps due to a sense of helplessness in the face of what cannot be seen. The ninja night warrior, operating in the blackness of the unseen portion of the environment, therefore, becomes the unseen object of the enemy's fear. The ninja, materializing from the invisibility provided by the darkness, has the opportunity of initiating the action. The sentry, watchman, or patrol is limited to watching, waiting, and finally reacting, because of the constrictions of a purely defensive approach to handling the danger.

The following guidelines should be observed during training for night work in home or enemy territory:

- Darkness provides concealment, but not protection or cover. Be aware of the possibility of random bullets or grenades that could be launched in your direction.
- Darkness does not guarantee total invisibility. Be aware of the possibility of infrared, laser, or heat sensitive optical devices being used to spot you.
- Due to the internal structure of the human eye, it is difficult to see objects in low-light conditions by looking directly at them. Glance around the object with quick, flitting eye motions, look out of the corner of your eyes, or lift your gaze above the object in order to use your eyes to best advantage during night operations.
- The process of fully adapting the eyes from a light environment to darkness requires a minimum of twenty to thirty minutes. However, to adjust from a dark environment to bright surroundings takes less than a minute. A bright flash or spotlight is all that it takes to break down your night vision, thereby causing the slow adaptive process to begin all over again for effective operation in the darkness. Be aware that a guard or sentry sitting at a lighted watch post or campfire will have greatly reduced vision capabilities when looking away from the light to peer into the darkness in search of you.
- Avoid staring into white light, which quickly breaks down night vision. For night map reading, lock picking, or intelligence scanning, a small red lensed flashlight can be used in place of the undesirable white pool of light.
- Flares and searchlights instantly remove the cover of darkness. When caught by a ground flare, panning searchlight, or bonfire, dive out of the lighted area as quickly as possible. Aerial flares and helicopter-mounted searchlights can often be detected before they totally expose your area. On the other hand, when caught beneath an overhead floodlight or flare, freeze in position under a tree, inside a cliff overhang, or among rocks or uneven ground. In that situation, avoid attention-drawing motion as much as possible.
- When required to move across open areas, plan your route carefully. When exposed, move in quick bursts from shadow to shadow, cover to cover. In subdued or broken lighting, move slowly and steadily from spot to spot, or use one of the ninjutsu *taihenjutsu* rolling travel methods. Always be alert for alternate escape routes if escape should become necessary. If it is impossible to move without making noise, remember that short bounding or scurrying movements are closer to the patterns of night animals, and blend better with the natural night sounds than the paced rythmical motions typical of human movement.
- Use weather conditions as aids and not hindrances. Falling rain and dark cloud cover provides excellent shielding for night work. The noise of the rain conceals activity and the soft damp ground reduces the noise of footsteps. Moonlit nights are best suited for reconnaissance and observation, while moonless or overcast nights are better for covert infiltration, exfiltration, or combat action.
- Whenever practical, study your destination in as much thorough detail as possible before going in, so as to reduce the danger of getting lost or becoming confused inside the enemy's territory. Learn routines, landmarks, and general layouts. Pre-action scouting of territory as many times as possible cannot be overemphasized in its importance to the night warrior engaged in covert activ-

ity. Stay alert and sensitive to your relation to cardinal directions. Losing your sense of direction at night could result in a fatal mistake.

The ninja uses the realms of light and shadow as symbols of the ability to blend with, and move through, all aspects of nature, comfortable in the knowledge that by becoming one with the surroundings, one can vanish in the minds and eyes of pursuers. Light and darkness, heat and cold, mountain and valley, the four seasons, and the elements of nature all befriend the ninja who has attained the enlightened power of oneness with the universe.

GOTONPO

Historically, these natural escape strategies of ninjutsu were referred to by the title *gotonpo*, or "five elements concealing and escaping methods." The five symbolic elements were known as the *gogyo*, or "five elements transformations," and consisted of earth, water, fire, metal, and wood, each a symbol of a particular quality of "changing." The escape-and-concealment method consists of utilizing one of the elements as an appropriate mode of cover for escape and evasion. This tactic of invisibility through blending with nature does, however, involve far more than the symbolic code implied in the five elements title in its literal sense. The ninja warrior is expected to be able to move unhindered whenever and wherever necessary, no matter what the surroundings or prevailing environment.

As a guide to general combat and escape strategy, the *gogyo* five elements can be seen to represent the following tactical options:

1. *Mokutonjutsu* ("wood") represents rising, growing, swelling energy that could be employed to overcome the enemy's tendencies to rely on gathering, condensing, and stabilizing tactics. As an example of *mokutonjutsu* strategy, we could use the statement, "My forces marshal more troops and move against you with growing intensity as your forces attempt to hold onto your own territory."
2. *Katonjutsu* ("fire") represents expansive, evasive, free energy that could be utilized to

The *gogyo* "five element transformations" in their productive cycle, showing how one phase of energy manifestation leads naturally to another, and is seen thereby as producing the next stage of energy development. The labels of earth, metal, water, wood, and fire are used here as a form of code symbolism for the five energy transformation stages, and are not necessarily to be adhered to literally. "Water" sinking energy eventually produces "wood" upward growth energy. Upward rising energy eventually leads to "fire" free dissipated energy. Dissipation eventually begins to come together and draw down into "earth" solidity. Solidifying energy eventually produces the "metal" state of hardness. Hardness eventually cracks and dissolves into "water" melting, sinking energy. Through an intimate awareness of the inevitable cycle of nature, the ninja warrior came to be seen as having the mysterious ability to predict the future, when in reality he was scientifically reciting the most reliably predictable likelihood.

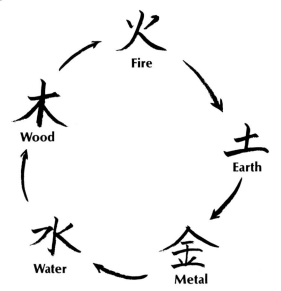

overcome the enemy's tendencies to rely on hard, edged, unbreakable tactics. As an example of *katonjutsu* strategy, we could use the statement, "My forces scatter and evade to frustrate and dissipate the power of your forces as they attempt to launch a piercing attack."
3. *Dotonjutsu* ("earth") represents gathering, condensing, and stabilizing energy that could be employed to overcome the enemy's tendencies to rely on melting, dissolving, and sinking tactics. As an example of *dotonjutsu* strategy, we could use the statement, "My forces draw together and intensify their hold on the territory as your forces attempt to slip in easily and surreptitiously."

The *gogyo* in their destructive cycle, showing how any given phase of energy manifestation can be inhibited or overcome by another, and is seen thereby as being destroyed. Again, it must be emphasized that the element labels are used as codes for understanding combat strategy, and are not necessarily limited to their literal reference to using nature for concealment and escape. "Fire" dissipation and free movement renders piercing and direct "metal" thrusts ineffective. Edged and direct "metal" advances nip growing and building "wood" energy in the bud. Growing and branching power breaks up "earth" contracting and ground-holding energy. "Earth" compacting and damming energy stops "water" sinking down and melting away energy. Sinking energy combats "fire" evasive free moving energy.

4. *Kintonjutsu* ("metal") represents hard, edged, unbreakable energy that could be utilized to overcome the enemy's tendencies to rely on rising, growing, swelling tactics. As an example of *kintonjutsu* strategy, we could use the statement, "My forces launch an immediate and decisive attack against your forces as they attempt to build strength and move into an advantageous position."

5. *Suitonjutsu* ("water") represents melting, dissolving, and sinking energy that could be utilized to overcome the enemy's tendencies to rely on expansive, evasive, free tactics. As an example of *suitonjutsu* strategy, we could use the statement, "My forces quietly melt into your territory as your forces scatter and thin out in an attempt to cover even more territory."

The ninja warrior using the tree for concealed observation of the enemy is merely symbolic of the *mokutonjutsu* "wood escape arts" of gaining the upper hand over the adversary who toils at holding his ground. The ninja's *gotonpo* "five elements of escape and evasion" is much more thorough and scientific than the simple teachings of hiding in trees, behind rocks, or within smoke clouds as is so often suggested in the books of authors who have not had the opportunity to actually experience the study of the authentic Japanese *shinobi* arts.

By becoming the earth and holding his position, the ninja thwarts the enemy who attempts to melt into the territory in search of him. The concealed warrior in this illustration is used as a symbol of the *dotonjutsu* "earth escape arts" that are much more far reaching in scope than the mere act of burrowing into the ground to escape hostile pursuers.

The submerged ninja breathing through a reed tube is symbolic of the *suitonjutsu* "water escape arts" of sinking out of sight to avoid the enemy who hastily scatters to cover the territory looking for him. Again, it must be emphasized that the gotonpo science of evasion is represented here in symbolism only. Mastery of the true art of invisibility requires an extensive knowledge and sensitivity towards the subtle vibrations of nature, the passing of the cycles, and an intuitive grasp of the enemy's psychology. Concealment under water has for centuries been used merely as a symbolic rendering of the teachings of one of the five branches of tactics.

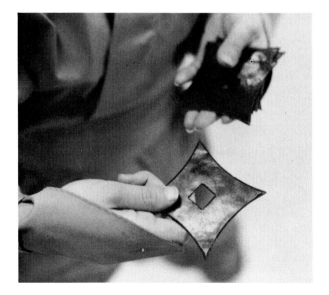

6
SHURIKEN
NINJA THROWING BLADES

Perhaps the most well-known weapon in the historical ninja's fighting arsenal is the *shuriken* throwing blade. At least as far as contemporary popular novels, movies, and television programs are concerned, nothing triggers thoughts of the ninja as readily as those flying blades of thin hammered steel. Though training shuriken can now be purchased conveniently from any of countless martial arts supply houses, it is ironic that the shuriken was once one of the most closely guarded secrets of certain ninja families of feudal Japan.

The Japanese written characters for the word shuriken include *shu* (hand), *ri* (release), *ken* (blade), for the quite literal description of "hand released blade." Historically, there were two fundamental blade designs. *Bo* shuriken were straight spike-like blades with either one or two pointed ends. A variation of the bo shuriken were *itaken* "board blades," which were flat bars of steel with one or two pointed ends. The second fundamental shuriken design concept was the *hira*, or "flat," shuriken, which were thin metal plates with anywhere from three to as many as eight points radiating out from the center. The *hira* shuriken were also sometimes referred to as *shaken*, or "wheel blades," because of their distinctive spoke-like shape.

Tracing back through history to determine the origins of the ninja's unique throwing weapon is difficult if not impossible. In theory, it can be seen how the four-pointed *senban* shuriken, characteristic of the Togakure ryu of ninjutsu, was perhaps developed from the four-cornered, iron reinforcing plates that backed up the heads of the spikes used in the joining of timbers in castle and fortress construction. Such blunt heavy throwing missiles were known as *tsubute*. By heating and hammering out the four-pointed reinforcing washer, it would be possible to form a thin flat blade that could be ground at the points for sharpness.

The ninja's eight-pointed *happo* shuriken could have likewise been developed from a source totally unrelated to weapon combat. One of the *nin-po mikkyo* ("secret knowledge" spiritual lore) ritual implements was a wheel-like device of eight spokes, representative of the eight-fold "wheel of cosmic law." Since the true ninja families of feudal Japan saw themselves as the tools of universal law, it would be highly likely that the symbol of the rimless wheel of law could be seen as an appropriate means of accomplishing the family's aims.

SHURIKEN TRAINING

As reflected in the literal translation of the word *shuriken* itself, learning the proper method of releasing the blade is the most important aspect

119

of shuriken throwing practice. To begin training with the throwing blades, whether the straight *bo* shuriken or the multipointed *hira* shuriken, it is crucial to first get used to the feel of correctly releasing the blade for accurate flight.

Begin your training by lightly tossing the blade straight into a wooden or Styrofoam target, without any concern whatsoever for distance or power. In this initial stage, the target itself does not need to be more than three or four feet away. Distance can be accommodated later, once a proper throw has been developed. Power will come naturally after that, as a product of experience and competence.

A light tensing of the fingers and wrist at the moment of release will create the proper feel for a straight and accurate throw. Work on developing the feeling that the blade seems to slip out of your hand by itself, rather than the feeling of flinging or slamming the shuriken into the target with the muscles of the arm. By allowing the blade to slip from your grasp at just the right instant, you cause the blade to cut through the air with the proper trajectory.

The star-shaped plate shuriken can be stacked in the left hand and slid off one at a time for throwing with the right hand. The shuriken are held on a horizontal plane in the palm of the left hand, and the outer edge of the right thumbtip catches in the shuriken's center hole to slide the blade off the stack and send it on its way to the target. This throwing method creates a rapid-fire succession of blade hits that can "track" the target as it moves toward you.

Straight spike or bar shuriken can be held in a bundle in the left hand and extracted one at a time for throwing with the right hand. The entire bundle can be lifted slightly with the left hand following the right hand as it draws the blade for each throw. The long narrow shuriken are held in the hand lightly, with the fingertips gently supporting the spike or bar in place for throwing.

Power and accuracy in shuriken throwing are generated by moving the body along with the throwing hand action. The body can rock back and forth, pulling back to ready each blade and rocking forward on the knees for each throw, or the rear foot can slide into forward position with the throw. The feeling of body weight behind the blade throwing action is similar to that of effectively using the body weight in motion to generate power for punches in the ninja's taijutsu unarmed combat method. Indeed, without a proper grounding in the principles of taijutsu, it is difficult to ever gain a combat mastery of the throwing blades.

The most common mistake encountered in shuriken practice throwing is the use of a flinging arm and a solid stance to project the missiles at their target. As the arm fans out horizontally across the midsection, the hand must release the blade at precisely the correct degree of the flat arc, with just the right timing, when throwing in this manner. This is extremely difficult, and can usually be accomplished only by standing in one spot and investing countless hours in unnecessary drill. In the heat of life-saving action, standing in one spot like a pub tournament dart thrower would most likely be a fatal mistake in tactics. It is much simpler to learn to throw by projecting the arm in a straight path with the moving body providing power and alignment accuracy, and therefore developing a much more reliable fighting skill with the ninja's shuriken.

When throwing the flat *hira* shuriken in fast multiple bursts, use the palm of the supporting hand to bring the stack of blades into position so that the thumb of the throwing hand can catch the center hole and slide the shuriken into the proper grip for throwing. With the thumb and first or second finger holding the outer edge of the point, the arm is extended to send the shuriken off with a saw-blade spin.

The process of throwing the flat shuriken for self-protection is one that blends actions of the eyes, breath, knees and ankles, torso, and, of course, arm and wrist. The body rocks forward with each throw to provide flying and cutting power to the blade. Avoid the futility of freezing the body in position and attempting to generate power from the arm alone. The body rocks back each time a new blade is taken into hand, so that the forward power motion can be set up for the next throw. Be sure to coordinate your breath with your body actions; pull air in with each return to ready position and push air out with each movement forward to release the blade. The overhand throw can be executed with either rocking or, as illustrated in the third throw on page 124, step-through footwork.

First Throw . . .

A

D

Second Throw . . .

A

B

B

C

E

C

D

Third Throw . . .

A

D

B

C

E

The shuriken held tightly in the hand for close range in-fighting claw-and-stab action can quickly be flipped over into position for throwing. The pointer and middle fingers tighten together and the thumb slides under for the subtle push that allows the diamond shaped shuriken to roll over the fingers and into throwing position with a light tumbling feel. As with all other skills in the ninja's self-protection arts, repetitious practice is required for combat-efficient mastery.

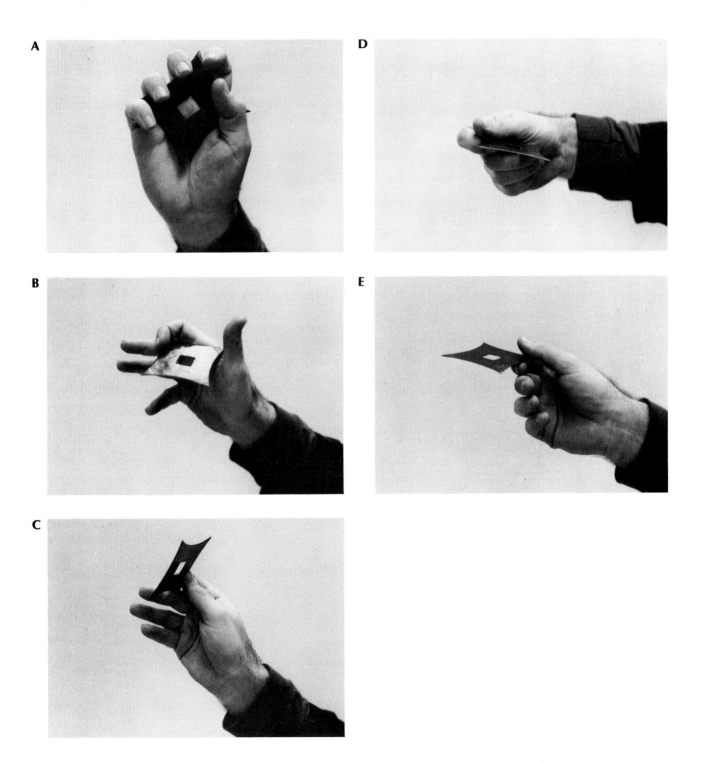

A

B

C

D

E

Distance Throwing

Once a proper feel for throwing has been developed, distance from the target can be increased. With the star-shaped *hira* shuriken, distance does not have much effect on the throwing method, in that the stars are thrown with a rapid spinning motion that facilitates cutting at any distance that can be thrown. The straight *bo* shuriken require much more attention when it comes to distance, however, because of the different throwing style employed.

At close distances the *bo* shuriken can be thrown straight into the target with no spin whatsoever. The spike blade is held point up in the hand along the extended fingers, and in effect slides out of the grasp and into the target surface with straight line trajectory. Beyond approximately three to four feet, depending on the type and length of blade and the skill of the thrower, the spike shuriken will begin to roll over end to end. At this transitional distance it is necessary to either slide closer to the target so that a straight throw can be used, or shift a little farther back so that a point-down grip can be used to allow for a 180-degree turning revolution in midair. This allows the blade to go from a handle-first release to point-first flight before impact with the target.

For close distances (up to 4 or 5 feet), the point-up grip is used.

again change the grip of the blade to a position with the point sticking up along the extended fingers. This grip and release allows the blade to go through a complete 360-degree revolution on its way to the target. A similar reversion to the handle-up position for a 540-degree revolution will be necessary when the distance increases to a range of seventeen to twenty feet from the target.

Obviously, plenty of repetitious training is necessary for mastery of the straight throwing spike, due to the wide range of variables to be encountered in any situation where blade throwing is required. Experience is the key to competency and confidence, because only by accomplishing successful results over and over again can true and reliable skill be developed.

The proper grip for the straight spike-like *bo* shuriken allows the thin blade to rest in alignment with the fingers.

Again, as distance continues to increase, additional rolling dynamics continue to have their effect. At approximately twelve-to-fifteen feet, depending on the shape of the shuriken and the depth of the thrower's step, it will be necessary to

At slightly farther distances (4 to 7 feet), the point-down grip is needed. As the distance stretches out beyond 7 or 8 feet, the point-up grip is again utilized.

As with the diamond-shaped *hira* shuriken, throwing the straight spike *bo* shuriken can be accomplished with rocking or step-through body action. As you breathe out and rock forward, push (do not fling) your arm into position aiming directly at the spot on the target that you need to hit. If you release the blade just as your hand is brought into position in front of your target, the spike should fly straight out of your hand. Your throwing hand will still be in position pointing at the target even after your blade has sailed forward to penetrate the surface. If you notice your arm dropping and flying past the target after you release the blade, that means that you are flinging your arm as opposed to throwing your shuriken. (**Photos continued on pages 128–130.**)

First Throw . . .

A

B

C

D

E

F

Second Throw . . . A

B

C

D

E

Third Throw . . .

A

D

B

E

C

EFFECTS OF THE BLADE

Contrary to the dramatic lethal effects of thrown shuriken seen in the martial arts film fantasies that now often include a few ninja for suspense or terror, the shuriken was never historically a weapon of instant death. The small blades rarely had points long enough to achieve a deep enough penetration to reach the heart, nor enough heft to burrow their way through the thick bone slabs of the skull. Instead, the shuriken was used as a weapon of distraction or harassment, cutting and injuring, and thereby causing hesitancy in the intentions of attackers facing the ninja. In the days where body-and-limb armor was standard equipment for even line-duty samurai, effective targets for the small throwing blades were restricted to the hands, face, and neck.

Much has been written in the popular histories of the ninja and their secret fighting art about the use of various poisons used to coat the points and cutting edges of shuriken. It is highly likely that some use of poisons was studied and employed; however, the effects of even the most deadly of our current technology's toxins are far from instant. In actuality, one of the most effective poisons used to coat the shuriken blade in feudal Japan was common, ordinary rust. In the days long before the development of tetanus serum, the threat of a rusty blade slicing into the surface tissues of the body was literally a lethal promise to be avoided at any cost. Any guard who had lost a friend or associate to the effects of fever and delirium after being hit with a filthy spike or star would naturally hesitate before charging after what he knew to be sure death in the hands of the ninja he faced. This was often all the respite the ninja needed to make good his escape.

Another common misconception is the belief that it is necessary to "stick" the star shuriken in the target every time one is thrown. Contrary to popular belief, it is not always the best tactic to throw the *shaken* or *hira* shuriken in a manner that causes them to embed themselves in the target. The most commonly employed method for throwing in the past ages of Japanese history was to use a rapid spin which would cause a saw-like cut and then take the *shaken* away from its target. This method prevented the wounded adversary from pulling the blade from its nonlethal penetration and hurling it back at the ninja who had thrown it in the first place. When training with the star shuriken, control of the blade is the goal, not a target bristling with points every time. The training should be varied so that penetration and flying cut skills are developed side by side.

BLADE AVOIDANCE

As a means of learning how to defend against the thrown shuriken while also becoming aware of the vulnerabilities inherent in the throwing method, the student of the ninja's shurikenjutsu art must practice the skills of *totoku heishi*, or "the shielding sword that returns the onslaught." Taijutsu unarmed combat footwork, body dynamics, and angling are employed from behind a screen of the upraised *ninja-to* sword as a means of warding off an enemy's thrown shuriken and sending them back at their original thrower.

A variation of this defensive action is to use the ninja's taihenjutsu body-movement art as a means of avoiding the flying blades. The body is pulled out of the way of the shuriken's path at the last moment, or the flattened palm of the hand is used to smack the whirling star blades out of the air. Of course, care must be used when hitting the blades, so that the palm hits the flat side of the *hira* shuriken, and not the edge of the pointed blades.

Practice in this method begins with avoiding shuriken that are thrown with a slow-motion action and an aim for the centerline of the body. The student is encouraged to learn how to relax and move at the last possible moment so as to allow for unpredictable blade flights later when the training is accelerated into full combat speed. Tension and jerky movements are to be avoided, as fluid adaptive moves are the key to surviving such an attack. In highly advanced stages of practice, the moving sword blade actually flings the shaken back at the attacker who initially launched them.

Woodblock print of kabuki actor portraying the cultural stereotype of the ninja warrior wizard, employing one of the kuji-in finger weaving concentration aids to give vibrant life to his intentions, reflects the Japanese image of the ninja as a potent mind clouder of enemies.

7
SAIMINJUTSU
THE NINJA'S POWER
OF DIRECTING THE MIND

The historical lore of Japan's ninja night warriors is full of tales centering around seemingly fantastic abilities that reach far beyond the capabilities of normal mortals. Of course, the exaggerated tales are based on roots of reality, which were then nurtured into the flowering of myth and misunderstanding. Skills of becoming invisible, the power to transform shape, and methods of flying through time and space are perhaps the most common ninja legends.

In the land of the art's origin, another legend—that of being able to cloud the minds of others—is also just as prevalent. Tales from the history of the art of ninjutsu include numerous references to *saiminjutsu* (hypnotism), *kiaijutsu* (shout of intention as a weapon), *ju-jutsu* ("ten syllable power method," different in this case from the throwing martial art of similar name), and *kuji no ho* ("nine syllable protection method")—skills said to enable a ninja to accomplish what conventional warriors could only back away from.

In truth, these "mind clouding" arts are not so far from reality as some contemporary historians, critics, and scoffers would have readers believe. Though often attributed to feats of illusion and deception on the part of the ninja, these mental skills are instead just as real and valid a part of the total *nin-po* training regimen as are the physical lessons of unarmed combat, pragmatic weapons use, and wilderness survival skills.

Scientific validation of the techniques of saiminjutsu, or hypnotism as it is referred to in the Western world, is based on evidence available to us all in daily life. Saiminjutsu hypnotism, as taught in the practice of ninjutsu, is a matter of using suggestion from the five senses in combination with the realm of the creative imagination to affect the mind's standard perception of a given situation or condition. Through the use of sense cues and suggestions, the subconscious mind is programmed to take in and believe what is presented to it, which later results in a standard or automatic frame of reference through the active conscious mind. This process is seen at work daily in the socialization and moralization processes used by all societies to bring children into acceptable roles in the community. Through repetitive observation of adult behavior, media examples, religious traditions, political climate factors, and educational institution expectations, young children are routinely "hypnotized" into points of view that will facilitate their blending in with their fellow community members.

It can also be noted that this universal hypnotism process could produce both negative and positive results through the same identical mechanics, so pervasive is the power of the process. Just as one can come to see his or her world as a delightful adventure through realms of ever-expanding personal power, one could also come to see life as a struggle through dismal realms of toil, sin, and confusion. It all depends on what has been programmed previously, and the quality of the input that works its way into the open and waiting subconscious mind.

Counterprogramming years of steady, subtle influence takes a strong sense of personal discipline to permit continued reconstruction work without distraction, an actual desire to alter set perceptions, and a knowledge of how the programming came to work its effects in the first place, so that the same process can be rerun in a more positively directed manner. With these three elements in coordination—the body, thoughts, and will—it is left only to the imagination and time to determine just what and how much can be done by the individual.

In the Western world, there is usually a distinction made between what is described as self-hypnosis and the hypnosis of others. Perhaps closer to the oriental concept of the ninja's saiminjutsu is the attitude that there really is only so-called self-hypnosis, and that the hypnosis of others is, in truth, self-hypnosis being accomplished with assistance from another person. Without the will to be hypnotized, or at least without the active will to avoid the hypnotic state, hypnosis as such is not possible.

APPLICATIONS FOR SAIMINJUTSU

In contrast to classical zen-style meditation, hypnotism works with similar mechanics but with different applications and dynamics. In meditation, the practitioner attains the relaxed and aware inner-directed state and then shuts down the active mind in order to listen behind the subconscious. In hypnotism, the practitioner attains the relaxed and aware inner-directed state and then switches on the active mind in order to talk into the subconscious.

Often associated with the ninja's legendary abilities to direct or channel energy, consciousness, or awareness, saiminjutsu hypnosis is perhaps most often employed to alter the ninja's perspective or perception of any given current reality. In this application, the hypnotic process can be used in long-range fashion to slowly and steadily program oneself for desired increases in personal power, or can be used for timely immediate alteration of one's energy level, creative resources, or perspective.

Ninjutsu grandmaster Masaaki Hatsumi demonstrates an application of *kiaijutsu,* pinning the attacker in place through the sheer power of his concentrated intention in the form of a spirited shout. This form of controlling an attacker through focus of the mind and spirit cannot be taught or studied as such; the power can only be cultivated naturally through years of training experiences.

In another demonstration of *kiaijutsu,* the author's teacher uses a channeled intention in the form of a concentrated shout and lunge to stun and throw an attacker off balance.

A

B

C

D

In the Western world today, modern hypnotism seems to have developed a popular image as a last-ditch alternative for overcoming personal weaknesses such as the inability to stop smoking, lose weight, combat stress tension, or fall asleep at night. These lesser applications should not, however, blind the ninjutsu practitioner to the broader, more far-reaching possibilities of the ninja's saiminjutsu for assisting in times of dire crisis and life-threatening danger. Certainly, it is a good idea to begin one's saiminjutsu training by concentrating on smaller exercises that are easier to monitor for successful results. Success breeds success. This by no means suggests that the art be limited to these smaller applications in scope.

It should also be mentioned here that many fear the hypnotic process as a method of gaining improper control over innocent victims who are then forced beyond resistance to do the bidding of the controlling hypnotist. Like so much else from the art of ninjutsu that has been distorted beyond recognition by the entertainment press, the positive powers of saiminjutsu as well have been labeled as a form of coercive "brainwashing," to be avoided by the less than confident. Though there is the remote possibility that under extremely radical circumstances of total physical control over the victim, the hypnotic process could in time be used to undermine another person's well-being, such cases are extremely rare. The earlier reminder that one cannot be hypnotized against his or her active will is still the general rule that applies to the vast majority of cases.

An Elementary Exercise

As with the process of inward-directed meditation, fundamental hypnosis requires a relaxed physical state from which to progress into a useful and constructive mental visualization routine. Once the physical body has been relaxed and in effect "left behind," the various levels of mental consciousness are free to create the desired results through conditioning.

First find an appropriate place to begin practice in the ninja's saiminjutsu arts. Ideally, you should be somewhere private, where you have no fears of being interrupted by other persons, ringing telephones, or routine disturbances. If possible, pick a meaningful place that can be used again for future sessions, so you come to view the setting as special to you, as a place that reassures you that you have had, and will continue to have, successful results from your hypnotic training. Relax into a standard meditative seat with your legs crossed (if that is comfortable), sit against a wall with your back straightened, or stretch out on the floor or in a lounge chair. Be sure that you are wearing loose, comfortable clothing that does not restrict you in any way that could later cause a distraction by interfering with relaxed deep breathing. Unbuckle or untie your belt, unfasten buttons, and take off your shoes, any jewelry, or glasses. Shift or adjust your body position as necessary, and allow your muscles to unwind.

Once settled into position, allow your mind to let go of all directed or verbal thinking. Let your mind relax, putting aside all problems and mundane concerns for another time. Permit yourself to simply enjoy the experience of relaxing for its own sake.

Direct your gaze forward and slightly upward, as though you were looking at the point where the wall meets the ceiling while keeping your head level. While relaxing, be aware of the mild strain that this eye work exerts, and continue to hold your eyelids open. count backward from nine to zero, increasing your awareness of the feeling of heaviness in your eyelids with each decreasing number. By the count of one, you should barely be able to hold your eyes open if you are completely relaxed, and by zero your eyelids should lower almost of their own accord. While enjoying the feeling of rest that permeates your eyes, remind yourself that the rest of your body is also enjoying this same restfulness, and turn your thoughts inward to the realm of internal perceptions.

Become aware of your natural breathing cycles of inhalation and exhalation. You do not have to do anything specifically, just relax and be aware of the action of your lungs and the related muscles and bones that are affected by the breathing process. Breathe deeply and evenly from your diaphragm, allowing the breathing sensation to be felt all the way into your lower abdomen. With each lungful of air that you take in, remind yourself of the stimulating, positive, vibrational, energy that you are pulling into your system. With each exhalation of air, remind yourself of the heavy, negative polarity energy that you are releasing with the breath, and be aware of how much more relaxed your bones and muscles become with each breath you let go. Allow yourself to focus on the feeling of natural energy ebb and flow as you continue to monitor your own breathing for several repetitions.

Once you have become comfortable in your position for the exercise, allowed your eyes to close naturally, and set the pace for your breathing, the fourth step is to go on and release the last little bits of tension from your muscles, nerves, and circulatory system. Allow the image of "letting go" to take over your active mind as you begin to concentrate on total deep relaxation as a way to assist the mind in letting go of active external conscious activity. You might use a visualization of the tension in your body draining away just like water draining out of a soggy sponge, or dissipating off like the steam from a hot bowl of soup. Repeat the following relaxation routine in a leisurely manner in your mind, or tape it in your own voice for later playback on a cassette player:

"I feel myself relax and I allow my muscles to expand and release the last remaining vestiges of tension. I let go of all tension in my toes and feet. I feel my feet relax into delightful stillness as though I were in the middle of a deep and tranquil sleep. Now on up my legs, I feel the last little bits of tension fade away, leaving my calves and shins, and now my thighs, with a feeling of wonderful lifelessness, as though they were soft and supple clay. My hips and buttocks are heavy, relaxed, and their heaviness seems to melt right out and down into the surface that supports my body, I am so relaxed. I allow myself to let go of all lower body muscle tension and relax completely, just as though my feet, legs, and hips were delightfully beyond my active motor control. They are impossible to move, as though they belong to someone else, so relaxed am I."

Once you have gone through the first three steps of the set-up process, you have only to think the command and you will be aware of experiencing the feeling. Move on up through your body and continue the relaxation and settling process:

"My entire body trunk is relaxed and heavy. My back feels so open, wide, elongated, and relaxed, it is as though I were melting into the surface that supports my limp body. Each vertebra seems to relax and separate from the others as I let go from my hips up to my shoulders one vertebra at a time, relaxing all the muscles around each of those individual bones as I go."

Much tension is carried in the upper back, shoulders, and neck, so pay particular attention to relaxing these areas.

"My shoulders feel so heavy and wide, so relaxed, as I melt into the surface below me. I feel the muscles relax and let go of their hold on the bones of my shoulders and neck, and I enjoy the sensation of complete relaxation. Each vertebra of my neck separates from the others as I move up slowly from my shoulders to the back of my head. My scalp feels relaxed and loose, as I descend even further into the hypnotic awareness state. My face is relaxed now. All the small muscles around my eyes and mouth release their control, and my face feels as though it is melting into a smooth, calm surface."

Once you have achieved relaxation, allow yourself to maintain the feeling over your entire body for a few moments. Concentrate on experiencing the relaxed state from a total body standpoint. When the body is totally relaxed, it is difficult for the mind not to let go and relax along with the body. All the minor ramblings and chatterings of the mind are more easily brushed aside and let go. If some disruptive thought or mental attempt at surface-level consciousness should attempt to force itself on you, simply allow it to drop and fade away. Positive conscious direction always overcomes negative action in the mind, so avoid the futility of trying to "not think" those thoughts that pull you away from the goal you seek. Simply refocus on the state that you desire to maintain, and approach it from this deeper,

more timeless sense of universal intelligence.

After a few moments you will notice that your conscious mind seems to be floating around inside a body feeling of revitalized warmth and energy as you drift closer and closer to the very source center of your own life force. For a few moments, direct this life force sensation to any particularly troubling spots in your body. Areas of tension or distress can receive your attention as you imagine this well-being life force as a vibration, warmth, or color sensation that localizes in the area of uneasiness to provide relief. Again recall your breathing pattern code, seeing yourself as pulling in positive energy with each inhalation, and letting go and sending out the negative qualities from your body with each exhalation.

Directing the Energy of Concentration

To further hone and direct the energy of positive mental advancement, and to assist your conscious mind in its release of conventional past programming that holds you in negative or limiting self images, allow your imagination to take you even further away into its own realm. Picture yourself walking in the perfect land of peace and relaxed confidence for you. A beach at dawn, a country meadow on a clear summer afternoon, or a lofty mountain peak from which you can see for hundreds of miles are some suggestions for effective mental pictures of scenes that you could use in this next phase of the hypnotic process. The most effective scene for you is, of course, that place that provides you with the strongest impression of peace, contentment, personal power, and meaning in your own life. The more personal you can make it, the easier it will be to immerse yourself in the energy directing process.

No matter what you choose as your own scene, allow yourself to concentrate totally on all the sense impression details you can, in order to take your mind as far from daily reality and its familiar limitations as possible. As a suggestion for how to create a mental "place of power" for yourself, you can use the following description as a model:

"I see myself walking through a mountain forest of huge towering cedar trees. Far above my head, branches sway in the light summer wind, occasionally parting to allow the clear deep blue

In an illustration of merging with an attacker's intentions and thereby gaining control over his actions, the grandmaster of ninjutsu demonstrates an application of his *kukinage,* or "void and universal-energy throw", throughout which there is no need to even touch his attacker in order to throw him off balance. As with the other more advanced aspects of the ninja's saiminjutsu mind-controlling arts, the *kukinage* cannot be studied as a technique in and of itself; this throwing ability is the result of years of living the combat art's fundamental basic skills.

of the sky to peer through. The ascending path I seem to be following is ancient, worn smooth and wide by centuries of pilgrims and wisdom seekers who have climbed this way before me. Off to both sides of the path lie miles of the huge trees, their massive, maroon-barked trunks rooted in eternity and stretching skyward. At their bases, mounds of bright green mosses and ferns carpet the forest floor. The calling of crows and hawks echo and ring throughout the thousands of acres that make up this ancient wooded mountainside as I walk along in confidence and wonder."

The more realistic the image in your mind, the more potentially effective the exercise.

"I can smell, almost taste, the rich purity of the forest air as I take in and release each lungful of this enchanted air. With an increasing sense of the potential energy that permeates this special place, I continue to move smoothly along the path, going further and further into the heart of this timeless wooded tract. Occasionally now, weathered stone lanterns appear along the edge of the path. Tall and wind-worn white, their ridges and roofs are covered with the brilliant green moss of the ages."

You should now create a special and very personal place for transformation. The more detail you permit yourself, the easier and faster it will be for you to return on subsequent sessions. The following example is provided as a model for your own work:

"Far in the distance I can now begin to make out the image of a low building of some kind. As I continue along the forest path, the antique wooden structure comes more into view. I can now see that it is a classical Japanese structure, a seemingly ancient temple of gray weathered wood with an iron-colored clay tiled roof that slopes steeply upward. The building is tucked away and protected in the shadows of the trees overhead. Deep in the shadowy recesses of the wooden walkway that protrudes from the walls that seem to crouch beneath the huge overhanging roof, I can just barely make out a sliding panel door. I see myself walk up to the building, which I now recognize as my own personal dojo, or 'place for the study of the way to enlightenment.' I slowly move up the weathered stair steps to the door, which I find slightly ajar. I slide the door open effortlessly and enter the dojo."

See all the details of your special place with as much clarity and depth as possible. For the most effective results, immerse yourself in the process as deeply as you can.

"Once inside, I look around at the familiar surroundings, the same walls, the thick *tatami* reed mats that cover the floor, and far across the open space of the central room of the dojo and up on the central focus wall, the portraits of those persons of special influence and meaning in my life. It is comfortable here, and I know it to be a place of great insight and a source of great creativity and power for me. I walk to the center of the open training hall and sit comfortably, allowing the peace and serenity of the timeless atmosphere to sink into my relaxed awareness."

From this imagined position in your mind's place of power, you can go on to pose questions to the teacher you carry within yourself and know as your intuition, and then allow the answers to appear in your mind. You can direct your awareness toward creating or strengthening certain aspects of yourself. You can also work at reducing the effects of previous negative programming through positive image channeling. You can increase the effectiveness of recently acquired skills through positive visualization. You can effect self-generated healing actions for yourself or others. Your possibilities are as endless as your imagination is limitless.

Visualization

For the sake of this model of the hypnotic process, we will look at the exercise as a means of concentrating on attaining a particular goal. In this example case, we will use saiminjutsu visualization to create a positive mental picture to assist an imaginary student of the martial arts in the attainment of the goal of developing a weakened body structure into one of healthy, virile strength.

Continue the visualization process from your imagined position in your own personal place of power, in this case, the dojo structure mentioned previously. Instead of focusing on the previously experienced routine qualities of daily reality (physical weakness), allow your mind to create a moving sense experience of the desired reality (physical strength).

"I look down at my arms, torso, and legs, and see a perfectly proportioned body for a person of my height and sex. The body I see could be used as a model for the statues carved in tribute to the ancient Greek gods. I tense my arms slightly and see the muscle texture flex in potential strength. I twist my body trunk and watch the muscles of my abdomen ripple with fluid power. I stand before a full length mirror and observe the ultimate image of my own physical potential, and it looks perfect and totally appropriate to me. I turn around and grab a rope that hangs suspended from the beams of the dojo roof high overhead. With effortless ease, I climb up and down the rope several times, enjoying the sensation of my muscles and bones successfully carrying out the commands of my mind. I see myself drop back into a deep and drawn out defensive fighting posture and then spring forward like a wolf, the muscles of my legs and back as supple and strong as they can be. I drop to a prone push-up position and slowly perform the first of many deep dips and full arm extensions, thoroughly enjoying the sensation of my muscles working fluidly at my command. I continue on with more push-up exercises, knowing and feeling that I have the power to continue on like this for as long as I wish.''

Continue on with any other personal ideas of how it would feel to be physically strong, making each vision as graphically real as possible through the imagined experience of all five senses.

As an additional example of the hypnotic process in action, we can look at the procedure for overcoming a particular personal fear. In this case we will examine the method as it might be used by a student of the martial arts who has a great fear of speaking before groups of people or teaching other students at his own teacher's training hall. Once again as before, begin the visualization process from the point of settling into the center of your own personal place of power. In your mind's eye, create an experience of the reality you desire (confidence in self-expression) as a replacement of the previously experienced reality in daily life (fear of speaking to groups).

"I look out across several rows of faces turned in my direction. These are students who have come here expressly for the purpose of hearing what I have to say. I begin to speak to them about my experiences, and they all shift forward to hear, they are so engrossed in wanting to hear my story. As I complete my first few sentences, I begin to realize that I do have stories, knowledge, opinions, and feelings that are of interest to these people. The more I speak, the more confident I become. I enjoy the experience of expressing myself. My hands move with natural fluid gestures, emphasizing the meaning behind my words. My feet and legs carry me confidently and firmly about the stage area, the eyes of the audience following me raptly. My voice rises up from my abdomen, deep and rich in its tones, and confident in its pacing. I complete my presentation, and the crowd applauds enthusiastically, everyone jumping to their feet. I have enjoyed myself so much that I am surprised to see how quickly the time went by. Hands wave in the air to signal questions. As I confidently answer each question with surety and humor, I realize more and more that the audience accepts what I have to say at its own value. I feel no urgency to prove myself to these people, because I am confident in what I do know, and I realize that, of course, I have much yet to learn myself and there is no shame in that. I fully enjoy my lecturing experience and look forward to the opportunity when it next arises.''

Applying the Exercise for Results

The power of the mental image is in truth the source of all we eventually experience and come to know as reality in the so-called objective world of the senses. Beliefs that deal with reality are collected and assimilated over years of growing older, and therefore may take quite a bit of work to replace or even alter. Persistence is necessary if we wish to change a perception of reality that is based on childhood programming that taught us that we were weak, inferior, stupid, dirty, and sinful, or any other of the common mistruths that are forced on children by unthinking parents, schoolteachers, and religious authorities.

It is also important to note the power of the mind in determining just exactly what we as individuals will experience at any given point of life. If indeed we do not or cannot believe something, we will not see it. Therefore in applying the methods of the ninja's saiminjutsu to self or others, care must be taken to work within the subject's personal framework of what is possible and what is not. If in your own mind you firmly believe that you are not capable, or are not worthy, of healthy physical strength, the foregoing exercise in strength visualization would be of no avail to you. Your mind would reject the process by either not letting you see the images as they are described to you in the process, or by creating a feeling of foolishness, skepticism, or even ridicule toward the entire hypnosis method itself. You can use those signals as a warning that you are getting into areas that will require considerable work in order to have success.

In the beginning, it is a good general rule to work with one area exclusively, so that concentration and results can be monitored. Pick a skill or power that you know to be possible, and that you really want to effect in your life. You cannot "practice" the method and it is a bad idea to "play" with it; you actually have to use it. Also be aware of continuously reinforcing the programming during the rest of the day when you are not in the hypnotic state. Random defeatist thoughts such as "I want this to work, but I doubt it will," or, "With my luck, this is probably just a hopeless waste of time," or even worse, "This is ridiculous; who am I to expect to really become more powerful, skilled with a sword, calm in the face of danger, financially stable, etc." Watch out for those semi-conscious negative slips that work to reinforce the very weakness you claim to be removing. The mind in the present moment is the most potent tool for determining future perceptions of reality.

By himself, the author practices a kick, elbow and knee slam, and punch combination against a striking target at his outdoor training center. Despite the inaccurate fantasy image of the ninja as a supernatural wizard or a heartless assassin as perpetrated by exploitation films and magazines, the essence of the warrior tradition is the engagement of challenges for the purpose of experiencing accomplishment. The truth remains that the centuries old art, born of the need to overcome impossible odds against survival, continues to be taught as it has been handed down from master to student for dozens of generations.

AFTERWORD
NINJUTSU TRAINING OPPORTUNITIES

In the early 1980s, the once-secret arts of Japan's feudal ninja families first became available on a limited basis in the Western world. No longer considered to be a dangerous and illegal countercultural threat to the established government agencies of modern-day Japan, the art is now free to emerge into the light of contemporary society as a source for developing personal power, experiencing a vibrancy of living, and enjoying the harmony of body, mind, and spirit merging in effective synchronization with all other elements in the environment.

Unlike the majority of popular martial arts today, there are no sports competitions or aesthetic performance aspects involved in the practice of the authentic art of ninjutsu. The training itself is its own reward, and personal challenge spurring on personal accomplishment is the goal. The warrior ideal is still as valid today as it always has been throughout the saga of humankind.

The reader should be aware, however, of the unfortunate fact that there are very, very few legitimate teachers of the ninja warrior tradition in the world today. Once the art captured the imagination of the martial arts community following my return from apprenticeship in Japan, countless unqualified individuals have appeared to claim that they, too, are ninjutsu masters ready to separate the unsuspecting student from his money and self-respect. Before my return to the United States, no martial arts magazine had ever featured any reference to anyone teaching the authentic Japanese art of ninjutsu. It is, therefore, highly suspect that the current flood of "ninja teachers" now making their public debut have any credible licensing whatever.

The potential student of ninjutsu must bear in mind that there is no governmental agency regulating the teaching of the martial arts. Black sash belts can be purchased through the mail by anyone, regardless of training experience, and the only legal requirement for setting up shop as a ninjutsu instructor is a business license from the community. Unfortunately, all prospective students of the art must be warned to beware.

There is a grandmaster of the art in Japan, who is the recognized source of knowledge for those who would pursue the training path of the ninja in today's world, however. It is this grandmaster's influence that is reflected on the pages of this volume, and that oversees the training in the dojo network bearing his name around the world. Persons interested in becoming a part of the growth of the exciting life art of the ninja warriors in the modern age can write to the Shadows of Iga Ninja Society for information on membership in the society and inclusion in training seminars worldwide.

Shadows of Iga Ninja Society
PO Box 1947
Kettering, Ohio
45429-0947

INDEX

B

Bansenshukai ("Ten Thousand Rivers Collect in the Sea"), 4, 6, 7
Bo shuriken, 120, 126, 127–30
Blocking, 57
Bujinkan dojo ninja training halls, 12
Bujutsu, 1

C

Camouflage, techniques of, 102–13
Chokuto-style blade, 78
Chudan uchi middle-level hanbo strike, 58
Cigarette lighter, 55
Climbing skills, 110–11
Combat reality training, 11
Concealment, techniques of, 100–17
Cultural stereotyping, 2
Cutting, technique of, 82–99

D–F

Daijodan no kamae, 81, 86
Dotonjutsu ("earth"), 115–16
En no Gyoja, 8
Evasive movements, 20–29
Fajibayashi Nagato, 3
Fighting postures, 80–81
Forward breakfall, 48
Fujibayashi Yasutake, 4

Full standing forward breakfall, 49
Fu no kata. 11–29

G

Gakumon Gyoja, 112
Gando ("candle spotlights"), 55
Gedan no kamae, 81, 94
Gedanuchi lower-target hanbo strike, 58
Genjutsu, 6
Gogyo, 115
Gotonpo, 115–17
Grappling, 64–77

H

Hanbo half-staff, 56–57
    grappling, 64–77
    striking methods, 57–63
Happo shuriken, 119
Hasso no kamae, 8, 87
Hattori Hanzo, 2–3
Heiho military strategy, 1
Hira shuriken, 119, 120, 121, 122–24
Hojo Godaiki, 4
Honnoji no Hen, 2–3
Hypnotism, 132–34
    applications for, 134–47

I

Ichi no kamae, 81
Igabakama, 55
Iga-gumi organization, 2
Iga ryu ninjutsu, 6
Igasaki Dojun, 6–7
In-ton, 100–17
Invisibility, art of, 100–02
Invisible, physical methods of becoming, 102–15
Iranki, 6
Ishikawa Goemon, 3, 7
Itaken ("board blades"), 119

J

Jizurigedan no kamae, 80
Jodan uchi high level strike, 57
Jojubu staff and cane fighting, 1
Ju-jutsu ("ten syllable power method"), 133

K

Kain Doshi, 120
Kato Danjo, 6
Katonjutsu ("fire"), 115
Kiaijutsu ("art of harmonizing with universal force"), 1
Kiaijutsu ("shout of intention as weapon"), 133, 134, 135

Kibi no makibi, 101
Kido Yazaemon, 6
Kintonjutsu ("metal"), 116
Kokinwakashu, 7
Kocho no kamae, 80, 89
Kongo no kamae, 80, 90
Koppojutsu ("bone-damaging
    methods"), 64
Koshijutsu ("muscle- and organ-
    damaging methods"), 64
Koshizashi ("hip-held gun"), 5
Kuji no ho ("nine syllable protection
    method"), 133
Kukinage ("void and universal energy
    throw"), 138
Kumawaka, 7
Kusari-fundo weighted chain, 56
Kusarigama ("chain and sickle"), 55
Kyoketsu shoge ("ringed-cord-and-
    dagger skills"), 55-56

M

Masaaki Hatsumi, 1
Mashita Nagamori, 5
Mikkyo, 102
Mind, Ninja's power of directing the,
    132-41
Mochizuki Chiyome, 4
Mochizuki Moritoki, 4
Mokutonjutsu ("wood escape arts"),
    115, 116
Momochi Sandayu, 3
Momochi Tanba Yasumitsu, 3
Munenmuso no kamae, 62

N

Negoro ryu ninjutsu, 5
Nin, 1-2
Nin gu, 54-99
Ninja, 1
Ninja aruki, 31-53
*Ninja/Ninpo Gaho (Ninja and Ninpo
    Illustrated)*, 1
Ninjutsu, 7-9
    art of, 1
    development of, 1-2
    heroes of, 2-7
    training opportunities, 142-43
Nin-po, 1

Nin-po mikkyo ("secret knowledge"
    spiritual lore), 119
Noise, 31-32

O-P

Oda Nobunaga, 3, 5-6
Okinawan karate nunchaku, 56
*Omikoku Yoshiryaku (Brief History of
    Omi Province)*, 6
Onikudaki ("shoulder dislocating
    leverage"), 12
Onshinjutsu, 102
Patanjali, 102
Psychological factors, 114-15

R

Rekigaku study, 1
Robbaku Takayori, 5-6
Rokkaku Yoshitaka, 6
Ryusui no kamae, 81

S

Saiga Magoichi, 4-5
Saiga ryu ninjutsu, 4
Saminjutsu (hypnotism), 132-41
Samyama, 102
Seigan no kamae, 81, 88
Self-hypnosis, 134
Self-protection, 11
Senban shuriken, 119
Sengoku Tidai Warring States period,
    7, 9
Shadows of Iga Ninja Society, 143
Shaken ("wheel blades"), 119
Shaki no jutsu ("flag discarding"), 5
Shinobi shozoku, 55
Shinto ("divine spirit way"), animistic
    beliefs, 1
Shoten no jutsu ("vertical surface
    running"), 106-7
Shugendo, 102
Shuriken throwing star, 56, 118-31
    avoidance of blade, 131
    distance throwing, 126-30
    effects of blade, 131
    training, 119-20
Siddhis, 102
Sideways flowing body drop, 44-45
Sodezutsu, 55

Sonshi, 101
Sportsmanship, 11
Stealth training, 30-53
Stealth walking, guidelines for, 32
Striking methods, 57-63
Suginobo Minsan, 5
Sun Tzu's Art of War, 101
Sugitani Yototosugu, 5
Sugitani Zenjubo, 5-6
Suitonjutsu ("water"), 116-17
Survival training, 112
Sword, 78
    cutting, 82-99
    fighting postures, 80-81
    gripping the, 78-70

T

Tachi, 78
Tachinagara ("rear body drop"),
    46-47
Taihenjutsu, 114
Takeda Shingen, 6
Tanto, 56
Taruikada ("foot flotation pots"), 55
Tetsubishi ("caltrop spikes"), 55
Throwing blades, 118-31
Tokugawa Ieyasu, 2-3
Tools, of the Ninja, 54-99
Totoku heishi, 131
Toyotomi Hideyoshi, 5
Tsubogiri ("wall borers"), 55
Tsubute, 119
Tsuchiya Heihachiro, 6
Tsuda Minsan Kanmotsu, 5
Tsuda ryu *kajutsu*, 4
Tsugibune ("collapsible boat"), 55

U-Z

Uchidake ("firestarter"), 55
Uesugi Kenshin, 6
Upright flowing rear body drop,
    46-47
Vertical surface running, 106-7
Visualization, 139-40
Watanabe Hanzo, 2
Yamabuski, 1
Yari no Hanzo, 2
Yokonagara ("sideways flowing") body
    drop, 44-45
Zenpo ukemi ("forward breakfall"), 48